MW00783759

Chef Baba Cookbook
Eastern European Cuisine

By Miroslava Perge and Damir Perge

A Madman Interactive, LLC Book
DALLAS

Copyright © 2017 by Madman Interactive, LLC

Photography © by Madman Interactive, LLC

All rights reserved. No part of this book may be reproduced or transmitted in any form by any means, electronic, mechanical, photocopying, recording, or otherwise, without the prior written permission of the publisher. For information on getting permission for reprints and excerpts, contact info@madmaninteractive.com.

The Chef Baba Cookbook books is available for special promotions and premiums. For details, contact: Director, business development, Madman Interactive, info@ madmaninteractive.com

      Library of Congress Cataloging-in-Publication Data
Perge, Miroslava and Perge, Damir
      Chef Baba Cookbook / Miroslava Perge and Damir Perge; photography by Jana Arnold, Damir Perge, and Angela Perge—1st. ed.

      Includes Index.
      ISBN 978-0-9996984-1-9
      I. Cooking. I. Perge, Miroslava I. Perge, Damir II. Family III. Title.

Printed in the United States of America
First Edition

BOOK DESIGN BY MADMAN INTERACTIVE, LLC

Edited by Jana Arnold
A Madman Interactive, LLC book
Version 1.04-BW
Madman Interactive · Dallas, Texas USA
Publishers since 2012

Websites: chefbaba.com • madmaninteractive.com

MSRP: USA $24.95

Acknowledgements

I want to thank my children, Jelena, Dejan and Damir and their families for giving me the encouragement to share my cooking joy with all of you. I also want to thank my large family in America and Serbia. Special thanks from the bottom of my heart to my producer and publisher Jana Arnold. Without her relentless effort, this would not be possible. And of course, I want to thank my son Damir for being a cooking imbecile and to allow me to teach him how to cook. That tells you that it is never too late for anyone to learn something new.

To all of the Chef Baba fans, I want to thank you for your thousands of messages in supporting me in sharing my cooking secrets from the old country. Over the years, you have said many extremely kind words to me, so I will end it with this: I love you more.

—Lots and lots of hugs and kisses, Chef Baba

I want to thank Chef Baba for taking the time to teach me how to cook. Never in my wildest dreams did I think I would learn how to cook. That is so, so not me, I thought. Becoming less of a cooking imbecile is an ongoing process. One thing I know from playing soccer is that you only get better through plenty of practice along with expert advice. I now have the confidence to learn how to cook, only because I'm being coached by a world-class expert. I am happy to be part of the cultural knowledge transfer of Chef Baba's seventy-five years of cooking experience, and share it with the rest of the world. I am proud to be called Chef Baba's Sous Chef.

Chef Baba, I love you forever.

I also want to thank our producer and book publisher Jana Arnold for making the Chef Baba Cooking Show and Chef Baba Cookbook a reality. It would not have happened without you. Chef Baba and I are extremely grateful and thankful.

To all Chef Baba fans, I love you for inspiring and supporting my mother in her quest to share her cooking knowledge with you. It has been a humbling experience reading to Chef Baba your thousands and thousands of comments and emails, showing your love and support. If you recall from one of the episodes, she is anti-computer. However, she finally has an iPhone, at eighty-five years old. Now the question is who is going to teach her to use it so I don't have to type her social media updates for her.

—Love, Damir (Chef Baba Sous Chef)

TABLE OF CONTENTS

Gibanica   Lepinjice

Meat Crepes   Krofne

Baba's Famous Chicken   Ćevapčići
Noodle Soup

Sarma (before going into the oven)

Lamb Chops, Baba's Oven-Roasted Potato Wedges, and Baba's Magic Salad

Desserts

Baklava

Apricot Dumplings

Keks Torta

Vasina Torta

*"Super clean kitchen means
no one uses it."*

—Chef Baba, Season 1: Episode 1

Chef Baba

Chef Baba's History of Cooking

Seventy-five years of cooking and still cooking.

I was born on April 27th, 1932 in Sremska Mitrovica, Yugoslavia—the oldest of seven children. I grew up surrounded by history and tradition. Sremska Mitrovica was called Sirmium during the Roman times.

First mentioned in the 4th century BC and originally inhabited by Illyrians and Celts, Sirmium was conquered by the Romans in the 1st century BC and subsequently became the capital of Pannonia, a Roman province. In 294 AD, Sirmium was proclaimed one of four capitals of the Roman Empire. Sirmium and the modern city of Sremska Mitrovica are located on the Sava River. Sirmium had 100,000 inhabitants and was one of the largest cities of its time. Ammianus Marcellinus, a Roman soldier and historian (born c.325-330, died c.391-400), called it "the glorious mother of cities." Remains of Sirmium stand on the site of my modern-day city today. Archaeologists have found traces of organized human life on the site of Sirmium dating from 5,000 BC.[1]

I tell you this short history of my birthplace and where I grew up because some of the recipes in my cookbook are thousands of years old. I learned from my

1   Source: Wikipedia.

Sremska Mitrovica in the 1950s.

first eighty-five years of life that cooking and culture are intertwined. One cannot live fully without both.

The cooking traditions have been passed down through the generations. I learned to cook from my mama and she learned from her mama and so on. Because we lived on a farm and my parents had to work on the land all day, I began cooking for my siblings at the age of ten.

My father, Pavle Radojević, wanted a son but before he finally got one, my parents had Beba, Vida, Rada, Caca, Joja, and me. They finally hit pay dirt with Lili (Miloš) as the seventh child. So helping my mama cook was a big task. Out of hundreds of recipes, the first one my mama, Zlata, taught me was Gibanica.

My mama was not only a wonder-

Pigpen at the ranch in Sremska Mitrovica.

ful cook, but she was also the butcher of the family. My dad would chase a pig around the farm until it was exhausted. He would hold it down and my mama would kill the pig. I was like my father and could not even kill a chicken. A lady across the road from us, Baba Roza, would kill the chickens for me to cook. My mama was a true chef. Even when she was exhausted from working all day on the farm, at 8 or 9 in the evening, we could ask her to make something to eat and she would always say yes.

My grandfather owned the farm my parents lived on, and my father was in the middle of building our house, and had finished only one room, when he went to war in 1940. The seven of us lived in one room for those two years.

In 1942, my father returned home from a German work camp. He finished building our home, and in 1943 our little brother Lili was born. At that time German soldiers occupied two rooms of our home. To celebrate Lili's birth, the nice German soldiers gave us a Christmas tree. It was not our custom in the Orthodox Church to have Christmas trees. That was an American custom. I believe that was a sign that we would be moving to America in the future. And my brother Lili would later be the first of the siblings to emigrate to America in 1967.

Even throughout WWII my family always had food. We used what we had and we were satisfied. Everything was natural—more than organic. We had pigs, ducks, turkeys, milk cows, and a beautiful garden. We had fruit trees bearing Rainer cherries, sour cherries, pears, and plums. We grew corn, and beets (to make alcohol) and made our own cheese, and sour cream.

I later married and had children—a girl

Miroslava graduating from high school.

Helen and twin boys Dejan and Damir. Besides working on our farm, I held a job at a bank. My coworkers called me "Farmer Girl" because I supplied eggs, cheese, and meat. They would come to our house to buy a pig, which we would butcher for them to take home. It was quite a life—a large farm, large house, Hillman Chrysler, and most importantly a large family and many friends.

Because our farm was fifteen minutes from downtown Sremska Mitrovica, my sisters and their husbands often came to visit us. As each of their families added new children, the family gatherings grew bigger and bigger. As is the custom in our country, I would make a variety of appetizers, pastries and desserts for the occasions—dishes like Gibanica, Listići, Meat Crepes, Burek, Lepinjice, various strudels and apple pies. For big occasions like Christmas or New Years, I made a magnificent feast that included Sarma, Prebranac, roasted lamb and roasted pork.

The family gatherings grew large in a hurry because Vidosava "Vida" and her husband Edhem "Eda" Kadić had Goran and Gordana, Olivera "Beba" and her husband Petar "Pera" Radović had Dragan "Daško," Radmila "Rada" and her husband Veljko Vidović had Siniša "Sonny," Zagorka "Caca" and "Borislav "Bora" Nećak had Aleksandar "Saša" and Aleksandra "Sanja", Jovanka "Joja" and Sergije "Braca" Urukalo had Ana and Milan.

Miloš "Lili," 'Michael" and Nada Ra-

dojević had Goldie and Nina but they lived in America. Of course, we always invited friends and neighbors—so there

Caca Nećak, Beba Radović, Ivan Perge, Rada Vidović, Veljko Vidović, Miroslava Perge, Boško Radojević, Beba Radović and Pera Radojević.

Duško Radojević, Stana Radojević, Borislav Nećak, Pera Radović and Pera Ninković.

Braca Urukalo, Bora Nećak, Pera Radović, Pera Ninković, Zlata Radojević and Eda Kadić.

was a lot of cooking to do for the occasions. But cooking was always fun for me and I truly enjoyed cooking for my family and friends.

Baba Zlata Radojević with her grandchildren: Aleksandra Nećak, Damir Perge, Aleksandar Nećak, Siniša Vidović, Dejan Perge, Dragan Radović, Goran Kadić, Jelena Šijak, and Gordana Kadić.

Life is about change. And things were about to change. We could see that Socialism and Communism in Yugoslavia were falling apart. In 1973 my husband and I went to the U.S. to visit my parents and brother, who were already living there. We saw a better future in America and decided to move. We left everything.

In 1974, we flew from Belgrade to Chicago with only our luggage, our kids and some money in our pockets. My brother Lili and his wife Nada picked us up at the airport in their Buick Skylark. They had driven from Austin to Chicago (17 hours). Seven of us rode to Texas in the car, along with our luggage. In my lap I held my beautiful, wooden St. Nicholas carving. My suitcase contained my precious crystal ware, which I had carried

on the plane, and miraculously none was broken. The twins were eleven and my daughter Helen was seventeen. Moving was hardest for Helen—leaving all of her friends behind. The boys fit right in and picked up English quickly. For the first two years in America I could not find anything I wanted to put into my mouth to eat. In the 70s, America did not have Whole Foods Market, Central Market or organic food like today. I had been used to picking fruit directly from the tree just as it became ripe.

Miroslava "Mira" with her children, Damir, Jelena and Dejan.

We struggled living in America. I began to wonder why I left my nice home, job and friends to go off into the unknown. It was like God had set me down on the Earth and I did not know where

Chef Baba

I was. My brother Lili could see I was not happy in America. In 1978 he gave me an early birthday present—a ticket to Yugoslavia and back. He said, "Only when you are really free, call me." I went back to Yugoslavia and saw my friends, and realized it was no longer my country because the economic and political conditions were rapidly changing. After 48 hours in Yugoslavia I called my brother to say, "I am free like a bird. Thank you very much. I know now where my home is."

Our first few years in America, we lived in a tiny house and kept chickens in the back yard. My father had a farm outside of Dallas and would give us a pig every year for Christmas. One year my husband had built a smokehouse in our yard, for sausage and ham. A woman knocked on our door one afternoon and said, "Do you know you have something burning in your house?" I explained that we smoked meat and invited her in to show her. She was delighted with our self-sufficiency. We had a rooster and five chickens so we never bought eggs. We had a pecan tree, and the rooster loved eating the pecans. When we killed him for the soup, he was as big as a turkey and it was the best soup we ever had.

I have returned to Yugoslavia only three times: in 1987, 1990 and 2000. In 1990 I went through Europe with my brother, to Germany, Hungary, Yugoslavia, Italy, and France. The civil war started in Yugoslavia in 1990. In 2000 my daughter talked me into going to my

Caca, Bora, and Sanja Nećak, Ana Urukalo, Miroslava Perge, Vida Kadić, Braca and Milan Urukalo before the Perge family left for America in 1974.

50th high school reunion and it was one of the best times I've had in my life. Sadly, now 75% of my high school friends have passed away. Our class had only 30 students and we all shared two pairs of sneakers and five to ten pairs of socks for our gym class. When I was at the reunion it was like we were all one person. It is difficult to explain that special kind of friendship. I don't think friendships like that exist anymore.

I was 41 years in Yugoslavia and now 42 years in America. I have truly had two lives. They have been two extremely different lives and I would not change either of them for anything—but both of my lives share two common things: my love for my family and my love for cooking.

Prijatno with lots of love,

—Miroslava "Mira" Perge

Mira in elementary school (1941).

Mira and her sister Caca working on the farm.

Mira's high school graduation (1950).

Mira and Ivan visiting Sarajevo.

Ivan working on the Ranč.

Mira in front of the railroad tracks in Sremska Mitrovica.

Mira's husband Ivan—Yugoslavian weightlifting champion.

Ivan teaching Dejan and Damir to play football (soccer) (1966).

The farm had pigs, chickens, and cows.

Baba's garden in Yugoslavia. A small portion of it.

Mira with her twin boys, Dejan and Damir.

Welcome home party for Chef Baba's mother, Zlata Radojević.

The Perge family in front of the Ranč.

Damir, Jelena and Dejan (1969).

Ivan conducting engineering survey for the water infrastructure.

The farm was called the "Ranč" by the Radojević family.

Mira with family before leaving for America (1974).

The Perge family leaves for America (1974).

Ivan and Uncle Joe Davis making sausage in America (1976).

Celebrating in America: Baba Zlata, Ivan, Dejan, Lili, Nada, Damir and Nina (1976).

Ivan, Mira and her mother Zlata eating a Balkan feast.

Mira and her dad's Husky on the farm in America (1976).

Lili Radojević, Rosalie Davis and Ivan Perge lighting up the cake.

Mira, Helen "Cica" Šijak and Siniša "Sonny" Vidović.

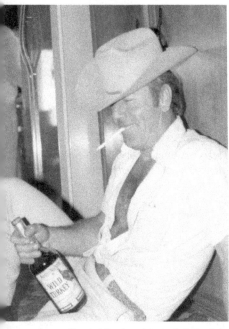

Ivan thought about modeling for Marlboro or Wild Turkey.

Ivan, Vida Kadić, Damir, Dejan "Danny" and Jelena "Helen" about to start eating at their home in Richardson, Texas.

Pavle and Zlata Radojević, Chef Baba's parents, with Goldie, Jelena and Damir.

What would a party be without Chicken Noodle Soup?

What would a party be without Gibanica?

Baba Zlata, Mira and Ivan working in the garden.

If you've seen her cooking show, you know Chef Baba is a huge fan of pigs.

Lili, Vida and Mira arguing about who made the best chili.

The siblings with their mother Zlata: Jovanka Urukalo, Olivera Radović, Zagorka Nećak, Michael Radojević, Miroslava Perge, Vidosava Kadić and Radmila Vidović.

Ivan wishes he was a Cowboy.

Family party at Lili and Nada's house in Austin. The table goes on forever.

At least two cakes are present at every birthday party.

Pigs are Chef Baba's favorite animals. Her father Pavle "Paja" was a pig farmer. Deda Paja with Nina.

Goca, Goran and Ana horsing around.

Appetizers

In Eastern Europe, the word appetizer does not fully describe these dishes because they could end up being all you need to satisfy your stomach. Gibanica can be eaten as an appetizer, side dish or main course.

When my husband passed away, my son Damir finally realized I won't live forever. He always never listens. For fifteen years I've told him I won't be around much longer because that is what all "Babas" tell their children, grandchildren, and great grandchildren. That is Serbian humor.

After seeing his father go to heaven, the first thing Damir asked himself was, "Who's going to do the cooking when Baba is gone?"

Damir tricked me into making the Chef Baba Cooking show. One day he casually asked me if he could record me making my Gibanica recipe that has been in my family for hundreds of years.

He said he wanted to carry on the cultural traditions after I was gone.

Because Damir was a cooking imbecile, he wanted to record the recipe on video so he could later share it with his children and grandchildren—and then have them make Gibanica for him.

After he recorded it, he realized these traditional Eastern European recipes were meant to be shared with the world. The rest is history. I share this first recipe with you from the bottom of my heart with great joy.

—Love, Chef Baba

p.s. Damir actually learned to make Gibanica himself.

Gibanica

This delicious cheese dish is perfect as a main entrée, side dish or appetizer.

- Season 1: Episode 1
- Preparation time: 20 minutes
- Baking Time: 45 to 50 minutes
- Serves 10 to 12

Ingredients:

2 pounds of cottage cheese
2 (8-ounce) packages cream cheese
1 teaspoon salt
4 eggs
6 ounces olive oil
8 ounces milk
4 ounces club soda
1 package filo dough (thawed)
3 tablespoons water
1 tablespoon olive oil

Instructions:

1. Combine the cottage cheese and cream cheese in a large bowl. Mix thoroughly with a fork. Mix in the salt. Mix in the eggs, one at a time. Mix in 6 ounces of olive oil. Mix in the milk. Mix in the club soda.

2. Drizzle olive oil on the bottom of a 14-inch round, 3" deep aluminum cake pan. Spread 4 filo dough leaves across the bottom of the pan, covering the bottom and sides—the dough leaves should extend 1 to 2 inches outside of the edges pan.

3. Set aside 4 filo dough leaves. Place the remaining filo dough leaves, one at a time, into the egg mixture. Wad and coat thoroughly with the egg mixture. Place as wads, into the pan, one at a time, covering the bottom and layering evenly. Pour the remaining egg mixture over the top. Fold the extended filo dough edges in, over egg mixture.

4. Spread 3 of the remaining filo dough leaves over the top to form a top crust.

5. Add 3 tablespoons of water to the bowl and mix with the remaining egg mixture residue. Sprinkle part of the mixture over the top crust, spreading with your hand to evenly moisten the filo dough.

6. Place the last filo dough leaf across the top, folding the edges inward to form a crust. Smooth a little more water/egg mix over the top filo dough leaf. Using a spoon, drizzle 1 tablespoon of olive oil over top. Allow the dish to settle for 15 minutes.

7. Bake at 375 for 45 to 50 minutes. You will smell the Gibanica when it is done and the top of crust will be a beautiful golden brown. Cut and serve warm or enjoy cold. If you have any leftover, refrigerate. Reheat in the microwave for about 20 seconds on high. Enjoy!

In our first ChefBaba Cooking Show episode, Damir introduces his favorite chef in the world—Chef Baba.

Damir and Baba argue about how to explain Baba's measurements.

Baba teaches her cooking imbecile son how to place the square filo dough into the 14" round pan.

Damir discovers making Gibanica is not as hard as he realized. "Hey, anyone can do this, even after drinking lots of Šljivovica," he says.

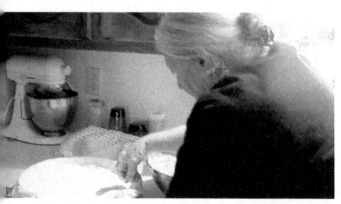

Baba teaches Damir the nuances of placing the egg and cheese mixture evenly across the round pan.

"Why didn't you teach me to make this 30 years ago?" asks Damir. Baba threatens to spank him with her large wooden spoon for being a smarty pants like his father.

Let the dish settle for 15 minutes. Bake at 375 for 45 to 50 minutes.

Fresh out of the oven, the crust should be golden brown. Ivan, Baba's great grandson, is a "Gibanica monster."

Baba watches Damir claim the outside edges of the Gibanica. When it comes to Gibanica, he can be greedy.

The Gibanica disappears within minutes around Chef Baba's family. They are never satisfied. She can never make enough.

When my twin boys were growing up in America, meat crepes were the one hearty appetizer that kept them going after playing soccer for hours every day.

It was not unusual for Dejan "Danny" and Damir to each consume 5 to 10 meat crepes before I could blink an eye.

It brought me great joy to make this wonderful dish for them, but I had to watch them like a hawk when making them.

One day I had made at least 70 crepes. I went to the other side of the kitchen to make the rest of the dinner before I started rolling the crepes with meat in order to fry. They snuck in on the other side of the kitchen and consumed 15 to 20 crepes each within minutes. They were lucky I did not skin them like a pig.

If you had been there, you would have heard a lot of loud Yugoslavian-style yelling and screaming. But deep down inside, I was so happy that they loved my cooking.

—Love, Chef Baba

Meat Crepes

This delicious appetizer is hearty enough for a meal. The crepes can be enjoyed separately as a dessert, with ground nuts and preserved.

- Season 1: Episode 3
- Preparation time: 30 minutes
- Cooking Time: 60 minutes
- Makes 20 crepes

Meat Stuffing Ingredients:

1 onion
1 tablespoon olive oil
1 pound ground beef (other ground meat)
1 pinch of salt
1 pinch of ground black pepper

Meat Stuffing Instructions:

1. Dice the onion. Add to a large pan with the olive oil and sauté over medium-high until the onions begin to brown.

2. Add the meat and mix into the onions. Reduce the heat to medium and continue cooking, turning meat as needed so it is evenly cooked. Add a pinch of salt and a pinch of ground pepper and continue cooking. Taste and add more salt and pepper if desired.

3. Continue cooking until the juices are reduced and the meat is cooked through. Drain off any excess juices from the meat. Set the meat aside while you make the crepes.

Making thin crepes is an art. The thinner the crepes, the better for meat crepes.

Crepes Ingredients:

4 eggs
2 ¾ full cups of whole milk
1 cup of water
2 ¾ cups of all-purpose flour

Crepes Instructions:

1. Add the eggs and flour into a large bowl. Stir, and slowly add milk, mixing with a fork or electric mixer. Add water and continue mixing until smooth.

2. Spray the crepe pan with vegetable oil as needed. When the pan is hot, add a ¼ cup of batter to the pan, swirling pan to smooth batter evenly.

3. Cook until the edges begin to brown. Flip the crepe over and cook a few more seconds. Slide each crepe onto a plate, making a stack, to cool.

Frying the Meat Crepes Ingredients:

> 8 ounces Egg Beaters
> 2 ounces whole milk
> 4 cups Progresso bread crumbs
> (plain)
> Olive oil

Frying Instructions:

1. Place a spoonful of meat onto each crepe and roll tightly, like a burrito, tucking in the ends. Stack them on a plate. After all crepes are rolled, pour Egg Beaters and milk into a bowl, and stir. Place bread crumbs in another bowl.

2. One at a time, dip each rolled crepe into the Egg Beaters, coating all sides. Quickly dip into the breadcrumbs on all sides. Place on a platter.

3. Heat the olive oil (2" deep) in a large skillet over medium-high. When hot, add a few crepes at a time, but do not crowd them. Fry until golden brown, turning so all sides are browned. Remove from oil and place on a paper towel. Serve hot or cold.

Baba teaches her cooking imbecile son how to cut onions for the meat stuffing part of the process.

Baba continues cooking until juices are reduced and meat is cooked through.

Baba and Damir argue about the measurements and how to explain " a pinch of salt" to the viewers.

Chef Baba

Baba teaches Damir to add a little cooking spray on the crepe pan as needed. When the pan is hot, she adds a ladle of batter to the pan while swirling the pan to smooth the batter evenly.

Baba instructs Damir to put a spoonful of meat into each crepe and roll it like a burrito, very tight. If you don't do this right, the meat will disperse during the frying process.

Damir finishes rolling the crepes with meat.

Damir learns to dip each rolled crepe into the Eggbeater, coating all sides. He quickly dips them into the breadcrumbs.

Baba heats olive oil in a skillet over medium-high heat. When hot, she adds a few crepes at a time, but does not crowd them. She fries until golden brown, turning so all sides are browned.

Baba tells the story about the incredible appetite her twin boys had when they were teenagers.

Meat Crepes   19

Burek with Spinach

A delicious and light version of the traditional burek enjoyed throughout Eastern Europe. Enjoy as an appetizer or part of a traditional dinner.

- Season 5
- Preparation Time: 20 minutes
- Cooking Time: 35 to 45 minutes
- Serves: 8 to 10

Ingredients:

1 package (1 lbs.) filo dough
(Baba prefers Apollo Filo Dough
No. 7)
1 package (10 oz.) fresh spinach
1 ¼ cup (10 oz.) farmers cheese
4 eggs
3 to 4 tablespoons sour cream
1 teaspoon salt (or Vegeta)
½ cup club soda
½ cup milk
½ cup vegetable oil
Dash of salt

Instructions:

1. Preheat oven to 375 degrees.

2. Wash the spinach well and remove the stems. Allow to dry. Cut the spinach into very thin strips. Place the spinach in a large mixing bowl, along with the farmers cheese, eggs, sour cream, salt, club soda, milk and vegetable oil. Mix thoroughly.

Burek ingredients.

3. Oil the bottom of a 15" x 11 ½" pan very well. Line the bottom of the pan with 4 filo dough sheets, allowing the edges to extend past the rim of the pan about 1" to 1 ½".

4. Add one filo dough sheet at a time to the spinach mixture and coat thoroughly. Place the wadded filo dough sheet in the pan. Continue the process until you have 3 filo dough sheets left.

5. To form the top crust, add the last 3 filo dough sheets, one at a time. Sprinkle oil on top of each sheet as you add them. Fold in the filo dough edges to form an outside crust.

6. Bake at 375 degrees for 35 to 45 minutes. The burek is ready when the top is lightly browned, and the edges begin to pull away from the pan.

Baba mixes together the cheese, eggs, sour cream (optional) and salt.

Baba loves to use the brand Kore from Bosnia for filo dough.

Baba oils the bottom of a pan. She lines the bottom with 2 or 3 filo dough sheets.

Baba brushes well with cooking oil, and club soda. Adds dabs of the cheese mixture.

Baba adds another layer of 2 filo dough sheets, oil and club soda. Repeats until she uses all filo dough.

Baba brushes the top layer of 2 filo dough sheets with club soda and vegetable oil.

Burek with Cheese

A traditional dish enjoyed throughout Eastern Europe. Enjoy as an appetizer or part of a traditional dinner. Layers of filo dough and cheeses blend together perfectly.

- Season 5
- Preparation Time: 30 minutes
- Cooking Time: 35 to 45 minutes
- Serves: 8 to 10

Ingredients:

1 package (1 lbs.) filo dough (Baba prefers Apollo Filo Dough No. 7)
1 pound farmer's cheese, cottage cheese, Greek cheese or combination
2 eggs
2 tablespoons sour cream (add if cheese is dry)
1 teaspoon salt
1 cup club soda
1/3 cup vegetable oil
Dash of salt

Instructions:

1. Preheat oven to 375 degrees.

2. Mix together the cheese, eggs, sour cream (optional), and salt.

3. Oil the bottom of an aluminum pan, approximately 15" x 11 ½". Line the bottom of the pan with 2 or 3 filo dough sheets, so the bottom is completely covered. Fold in the edges of the dough sheets.

Baba bakes it for 35 to 45 minutes. The Burek is ready when the top is lightly browned.

4. Brush well with cooking oil, and club soda. Add dabs of the cheese mixture. Add another layer of 2 filo dough sheets, oil and club soda. Repeat until you use all filo dough. Brush the top layer of 2 filo dough sheets with club soda and vegetable oil. Allow to set while the oven is preheated.

5. Preheat oven to 375.

6. Bake for 35 to 45 minutes. The Burek is ready when the top is lightly browned, and the edges begin to pull away from the pan.

Chef Baba prepares to fry Listiće.

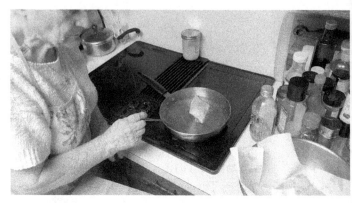

Chef Baba has made Listiće at least a thousand times for her family. And that is an understatement.

When they are fried, Listići puff up a little bit, making them so delicious.

Ivan, Chef Baba's great grandson, can't wait to get his share of the Listići.

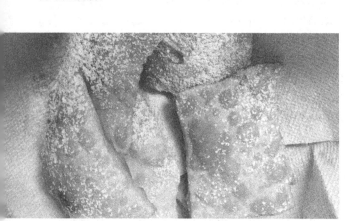

Listići are light to eat, complete delight to your stomach.

Breads and Pastries

Mouth-watering, stomach delights, from Listići
to Lepinjice to Krofne to Kiflice to Pogača. Yum,
Yummy, Babalicious.

Baba's son Dejan "Danny" climbs the old mansion back in Serbia with his former schoolmate friend Slobodan Crnjaković, and reminisces about the days when he and his brother would run across the internal beams. Definitely an extremely dangerous childhood activity.

Growing up in Yugoslavia was one of the best childhoods anyone could experience. My brother Dejan (Danny) and I have hundreds of stories of fun and mischief that we now share with our children.

I grew up on a large farm, which was a perfect playground. Our house was 50 meters from the railroad tracks. We often played around the train tracks and train cars. Next to our house was a partially-built mansion, which my grandfather was constructing when the Communists drove him out of Yugoslavia for being a capitalist. The mansion was 80% finished so it was a perfect place to play hide and seek and, most importantly, to climb and run along the beams that were ten feet off the ground. Obviously, we weren't allowed to play in the rafters, so we did it when our parents weren't looking.

Behind our house was a henhouse, a pigpen and a huge garden. The garden was surrounded by a barbed wire fence and a wooden gate that opened up to the street where we had on-demand access to kids in the neighborhood.

During the summer, we either played soccer in our front yard with our friends, climbed around the unfinished mansion, or played all kinds of games on the street outside the garden. It was not unusual for us to be out half the day playing with

our friends.

Our older sister Jelena babysat us during the summer while our parents worked—if you actually want to call it babysitting. We were usually out playing in the yard, the cornfields or on the street. My sister would make us a hearty breakfast of eggs, bacon and sausages, and it was normally accompanied by the freshly-baked Pogača bread my mom made.

At lunchtime, Dejan and I usually ran back to our summer kitchen to make ourselves a quick sandwich. This sandwich, unless you come from the Eastern European region, is quite unusual. We would spread lard over a slice of bread and sprinkle it with grounded paprika. The lard was light, and as white as snow. We loved the combination of Pogača, lard and paprika. Today, it seems like an odd and unhealthy thing to eat, but eating some natural fat is good for your body. If we were craving something sweet, we would take a piece of Pogača and spread it with homemade plum or apricot preserves. Super delicious.

Dejan and I could make our sandwiches in under a minute, and run back out to play, eating our sandwiches along the way. We often shared our Pogača delights with our friends. And believe me, sharing Chef Baba's Pogača with others was an easy way to make friends. And it is today. Try it yourself. Make Pogača and share it with your neighbors—even the ones you don't know. You will make new friends very quickly.

> —Love, Damir
> "Chef Baba's Sous Chef"

Dejan Perge at the Ranč in Yugoslavia.

Dejan "Danny" playing in the yard with a pig.

27

Pogača

This old-world bread recipe has been handed down for centuries in Baba's family. It is simple and rustic. Tear off a piece with your hands and dip it in olive oil, or drizzle with honey.

- Season 4: Episode 5
- Preparation Time: 15 minutes, plus 1 hour for dough to rise
- Cooking Time: 25 to 40 minutes
- Serves: 6 to 8

Ingredients:

8 cups all-purpose flour
   (Chef Baba uses King Arthur Flour)
2 packages of dry active yeast
1 teaspoon granulated sugar
3 tablespoons sunflower oil
1 cup milk
1 cup water
1 teaspoon salt

Instructions:

1. Place the flour in a large mixing bowl. Add the yeast on top of the flour. Add the sugar and the sunflower oil.

2. Combine the milk and water, and warm to about 100 to 110 degrees. Pour about ¼ cup of the liquid over the yeast to activate it. The yeast will begin to bubble. Sprinkle a pinch of salt over the flour surrounding the yeast, not over the bubbling yeast.

3. Gradually add the warm milk/water mixture as you mix the dough. Mix the dough with one hand, while holding the bowl with the other hand. Brace the bowl against your body to hold it in place.

4. Remove the dough from the bowl. Knead until smooth. If the dough begins to stick to your work surface, add a little flour to the surface. If the dough sticks to your hand, add flour to your hands. Continue kneading.

5. Place the dough in a 15" round pan. Cover with two towels, and let it set for 45 minutes to 1 hour. The dough will expand to double its size.

CHEF BABA TIP: Place the pan of dough inside your oven so it is not disturbed.

6. Remove the towels. Poke holes in the dough about ten times, using a fork.

7. Preheat the oven to 375.

8. Bake the pogača until the top is a beautiful, golden color and the edges pull away from the pan.

9. Remove the pogača from oven. Pat a little water on the top of the crust. Cover with a kitchen towel until ready to serve.

Baba teaches Damir, Jon Dylan (grandson) and Ivan (great grandson) one of the most traditional dishes in the Balkans. Baba places the flour in a large bowl.

She adds the yeast on top of the flour, then adds sugar and sunflower oil. Baba combines milk and water and warms it to about 100 to 110 degrees.

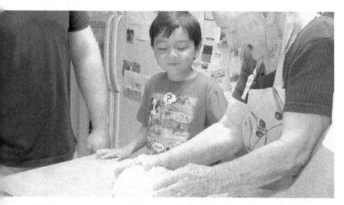

Baba pours about ¼ cup of the liquid over the yeast to activate it. The yeast begins to bubble. Baba sprinkles a pinch of salt over the flour surrounding the yeast.

Baba gradually adds the warm milk and water mixture. She removes the dough from the bowl and kneads it until smooth.

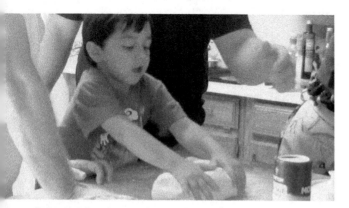

Baba teaches Ivan to knead the dough.

Baba places the dough in a 15" round aluminum pan, covers it with two towels until it expands to double its size, about an hour.

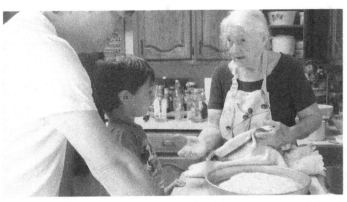

Baba removes the towels and shows Ivan and Damir how much the dough has expanded after an hour.

Baba pokes holes in the dough about ten times, using a fork, while Damir and Ivan observe. She preheats the oven to 375.

While waiting for Pogača to bake, Baba plays Tablići with Damir. Despite his prediction to beat her, she completely obliterates him.

After beating Damir in Tablići, Baba removes the Pogača from oven. She pats a little water on the top of the crust and covers it with a kitchen towel before serving.

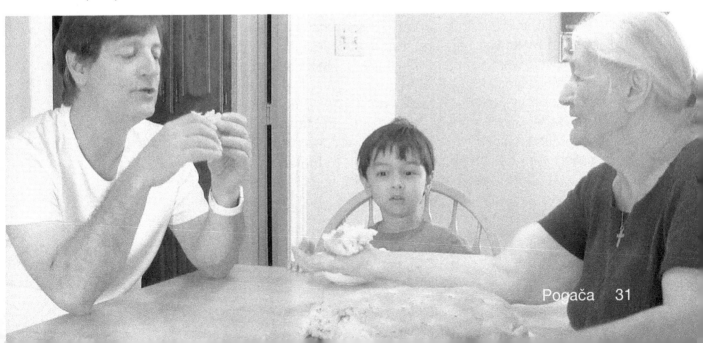

I don't know why, but each time I eat Lepinjice, I feel like a time traveler. It's crazy, but whenever I take a bite of this pastry, I feel like I am in the old Roman times.

Making Lepinjice is truly an art. They look easy to make but I assure you they are not—if you want to make them perfect. You truly have to know how to knead the dough or they just won't taste right.

Chef Baba, and I were both born in Sremska Mitrovica, Yugoslavia. The city was called Sirmium in the old Roman times ... so when I eat Lepinjice, I feel like a Roman emperor.

A quick Balkan history lesson: Sirmium was proclaimed one of the four capitals of the Roman Empire in 294 AD. Lepinjice is as traditional and Old World as you can get.

I have fond memories of eating Lepinjice during my elementary school days in Yugoslavia. I attended a school called Jovan Jovanović Zmaj. Every day during recess, the school served the students Lepinjice and yogurt. It tasted wonderful.

I truly believe that Lepinjice is served in heaven. Chef Baba makes the best Lepinjice. Period. I can never get enough of them.

I love you, Lepinjice—forever.
    —Love, Damir
        "Chef Baba's Sous Chef"

Lepinjice

These lightly fried Serbian doughnuts are served on the streets of Belgrade. They are versatile and can be part of a traditional Serbian dinner when served with Pasulj or Prebranac (beans), sausage and red pepper. Lepinjice is also delicious with powdered sugar or fruit preserves. This is truly a simple food that can even be made using only three ingredients: flour, yeast and water.

- Season 4: Episode 2
- Total Time to Make: 2 hours
- Makes 30, but how many it serves depends on whether Damir is present in the room.

Ingredients:

8 cups (1 kg.) all-purpose flour
2 packets dry yeast
(Baba suggests Fleishmann's Active Yeast)
1 pinch of sugar
1 ¼ cup milk
1 ¼ cup water
1 pinch of salt

Instructions:

1. Place the flour in a large mixing bowl. Add the yeast on top of the flour, and then the sugar on top of the yeast.

2. Warm the milk. In a separate container, combine the warm milk and water. Pour about ¼ cup of the liquid over the yeast to activate it. The yeast will begin to bubble. Sprinkle a pinch of salt over the flour surrounding the yeast, not over the bubbling yeast.

3. Gradually add the warm milk/water mixture over the yeast as you mix everything together with your hands.

CHEFBABA TIP: Mix the dough with one hand, while holding the bowl with the other hand. Brace the bowl against your body to hold it in place.

4. Continue adding the milk/water mixture until the dough is smooth. If you need more liquid add a little warm water, a teaspoon at a time. If the dough sticks to your hand, flour your hand and continue mixing.

5. Work the dough in the bowl by pulling it from underneath and toward you as you turn the bowl. Continue until smooth. If the dough sticks to the bowl, add a little flour underneath. Taste the dough to see if you want to add a little more salt.

CHEF BABA TIP: Make a little sign of the cross on the top of the dough for good luck.

6. Sprinkle a little flour on top. Cover the bowl with a towel and a small pillow (or two towels) in order to hold in the

warmth. Let the dough set for an hour to rise. It should expand to double in size.

7. Place the dough on a floured work surface and fold in half once. The dough will be light and fluffy. Using a rolling pin, roll the dough until it's about 1" thick. With a sharp knife, cut the dough into squares about 4" x 4", then cut a 1" to 1 ½" slit in the center of each and pull apart slightly, to form a doughnut shape. Set each lepinjice aside until all are cut.

8. Add olive oil to a skillet, about one finger deep. Heat over medium high until the oil is hot. Add two or three lepinjice at a time so they are not crowded in the pan. Fry until the doughnut expands and you see small bubbles forming around the edges of the dough. When the dough is lightly browned on the bottom, turn it over and fry the other side. Stack the lepinjice in a large bowl lined with paper towels to absorb any excess oil.

9. Serve with beans to make a meal, or sprinkle powdered sugar or a dollop of strawberry preserves.

Baba teaches Damir to make one his favorites. In a large mixing bowl, she adds the flour, yeast on top of the flour, and then the sugar on top of the yeast.

Baba combines the warm milk and water. Pours about ¼ cup of the liquid over the yeast to activate it.

Damir asks Baba if she has a bigger bowl than the one he is holding. Of course, he is just kidding.

Baba gradually adds the warm milk/water mixture over the yeast as she mixes everything together.

Baba continues adding liquid until the dough is smooth.

When the dough is smooth, she sprinkles a little flour on top. Covers the bowl with a towel and a small pillow (or a couple of towels) in order to hold in the warmth. Lets it rise for an hour.

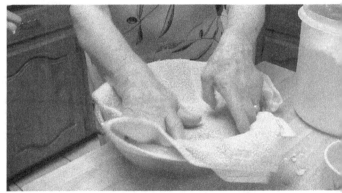

Baba covers the bowl with a towel and a small pillow (or a couple of towels) in order to hold in the warmth.

Baba explains to Damir that she lets it set for an hour to rise. (It should expand to double in size.)

No matter how many times she makes it, Baba loves to see the dough rise. It never ceases to bring her joy.

She places the dough on a floured work surface and folds in half once. The dough will be light and fluffy.

Using a rolling pin, Baba rolls the dough until it's about 1" thick.

Baba sprinkles flour while she rolls the dough.

With a sharp knife, cuts into squares about 4" x 4," then cuts a 1" to 1 ½" slit in the center of each and pulls apart slightly, to form a doughnut shape.

When the dough is lightly browned on the bottom, Baba turns it over and fries the other side.

Baba adds two or three lepinjice at a time so they do not touch in the pan. She fries until the doughnut expands and she sees bubbles around the edges of the dough.

Baba stacks Lepinjice in a large bowl lined with paper towels to absorb any excess oil.

Baba watches that Damir does not move to eat all the Lepinjice. It appears that Damir has already made his move for the first Lepinjica.

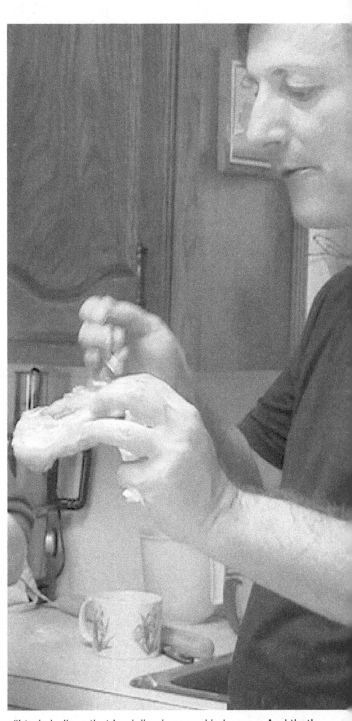

Lepinjice can be served with beans to make a meal, or sprinkled with powdered sugar or a dollop of strawberry preserves.

"I truly believe that Lepinjice is served in heaven. And that's just how I feel. I love you Lepinjice forever," said Damir.

Listići

Listići is the Serbian word for "leaves." This delicately-layered puffed pastry is served hot or cold with a dollop of fruit preserves.

- Season 2: Episode 5
- Preparation time: 1 hour
- Frying Time: 15 minutes
- Makes 40 to 60

Ingredients:

4 cups all-purpose flour
1 handful granulated sugar
1 pinch of salt
2 eggs
1 cup whole milk
1 cup water
4 heaping tablespoons shortening
   (Baba uses Crisco)
Light tasting olive oil, enough
   to be 1 ½" deep in skillet

Instructions:

1. Place the flour, sugar, salt, and eggs in a medium mixing bowl. Put the milk and water together in a large measuring cup. Gradually add the milk/water mixture as you mix the dough with your hand. Mix until smooth.

2. Lightly flour your work surface. If the dough sticks to the surface, add a little more flour. Form the dough into a loaf shape. Use a sharp knife to cut it into 4 or 5 equal parts. Knead each section

Ivo, just like his Deda, is also a Listići connoisseur. He can't get enough of them either. He's patiently waiting for his share of Listići with joyful anticipation.

of dough again, forming 4 or 5 smooth balls.

3. Use a rolling pin to roll one dough ball into a flat circle, turning the dough around frequently as you roll. Always roll from the middle, toward the edges of the dough. Roll each dough section into a smooth circle about 7" or 8" across.

4. Spread a heaping tablespoon of shortening across one dough circle. Stack the second dough circle on top and spread with shortening. Repeat until all dough circles are stacked on top of each other, with a layer of shortening between. Pinch the edges of the dough

together to seal in the shortening.

5. Use a rolling pin to smooth the entire stack of dough into a larger circle about ¼" thick or thinner. Gently rolling from the middle out in every direction. Make sure the edges are the same thickness as the middle. Add a little flour to the top of the dough as you roll, as needed to keep the rolling pin from sticking.

6. Use a round dough cutter to slice the dough into strips approximately 1 ½" x 4"—you can make them larger or smaller if you prefer. Place the dough pieces on a cloth as you cut them.

7. Add 2" of vegetable oil to a 3" deep skillet. Heat over high. The oil is ready when you can add a small piece of dough and it puffs up and turns brown.

8. Place the dough pieces into the hot oil, a few at a time so they are not over-lapped. Cook each piece, turning over, after browned on one side. Brown on the other side (about 3 or 4 seconds). Remove from pan and place on plate lined with paper towels.

9. Add a dollop of fruit preserves to the Listići and eat warm or cold.

CHEF BABA TIP: If you use lard, mix until fluffy before adding.

Baba adds the flour, sugar, salt, and eggs. Puts the milk and water together in a large measuring cup. She gradually adds the milk/water mixture as she mixes the dough. She mixes until smooth.

Baba lightly flours her work surface. She places the dough on the surface and kneads until smooth. Forms the dough into a loaf shape. Uses a sharp knife to cut it into 4 or 5 equal parts.

Damir uses a rolling pin to roll the dough into a flat circle, turning it frequently. Now, he prepares to slice the dough.

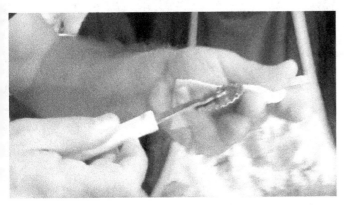

With a round cutter, Damir slices the dough into strips approximately 1 ½" x 4"—the size can vary. He places the dough pieces on a cloth to cut them.

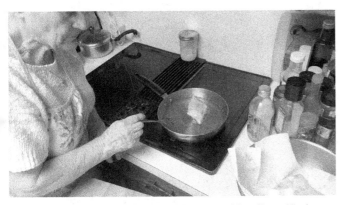

In a skillet, Baba adds vegetable oil to 2" deep. Heats it over high. (Oil is ready when you can add a small piece of dough and it puffs up and browns.)

Baba adds the dough pieces to the hot oil, a few at a time so they are not overlapped. She cooks each piece, turning over once, after it is browned on one side (about 3 or 4 seconds). Browns on the other side.

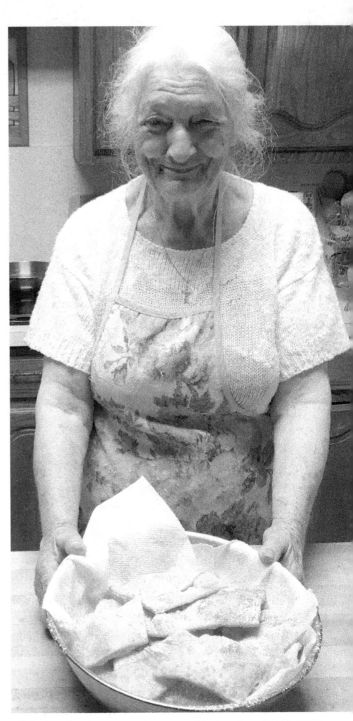

Baba smiles because she was able to stop Damir from eating every Listići before the rest of his family got to her house. They will thank her.

Chef Baba could never make enough of Krofne for everyone. These Serbian doughnuts are not like the doughnuts you might eat in America. They are not as sweet as American doughnuts, and I am more than fine with that because they have fewer calories. The name is derived from the German *Krapfen*, and they are similar to the Central European pastry *Berliner*. They are a close cousin to the *Beignets* served at the famous Café du Monde in the French Quarter of New Orleans.

As a good luck sign of prosperity, Krofne is served on New Year's Day and other special occasions such as Easter and Christmas. Chef Baba made Krofne more than only on special occasions, and she always told us, "I can never make enough for you." She is right. My brother and I were both known to eat at least 10 to 15 each.

What I love about Krofne is that you can DIY (do-it-yourself) improve on them by choosing what to put in the middle of this round pastry. Because of the way they are fried, the middle part of it is whiter than the rounded sides, making it a perfect spot for a dollop of jam or jelly. My favorite is strawberry jelly, sprinkled with powdered sugar.

—Love, Damir
      "Chef Baba's Sous Chef"

Krofne

Serbian airy doughnuts. Enjoy these delicate pastries hot and topped with your favorite fruit preserves and a dusting of powdered sugar. Children love to help make these too! These doughnuts are called by different names depending on the Balkan region: Krofne (Albanian, Bosnian), Krafne (Croatian), Krofi (Slovenian), крофне (Serbian).

- Season 2: Episode 2
- Preparation time: 3 hours
- Frying Time: 20 minutes
- Makes about 20

Ingredients:

2 cups warm milk
2 egg yolks
1 handful granulated sugar
1 pinch salt
1 tablespoon butter
1 pound all-purpose flour
1 package dry yeast
1 teaspoon granulated sugar
¼ to ⅓ cup all-purpose flour
1 (48 oz.) bottle canola oil

Damir uses powdered sugar to enhance his version of Krofne.

Instructions:

1. Combine the warm milk, egg yolks, sugar, salt and butter in large bowl. Mix with a wooden spoon until smooth. In a separate bowl, stir together the flour, dry yeast and sugar, then add to the first bowl. Stir 2 or 3 minutes until smooth – pulling dough toward you with the spoon as you turn the bowl. If the dough begins to stick to the bowl, sprinkle the sides of bowl with a little flour as you mix.

2. Cover the dough with a cloth, then place a small pillow on top to keep the dough warm as it rises. Allow the dough to set for about 1 hour, or until the dough doubles in size.

3. Sprinkle your work surface generously with flour. Lay the dough on the work surface, and sprinkle flour over it. Fold the dough in half once. Using a rolling pin, gently roll the dough until it is about 1 finger thick.

4. Cut the dough into circles using a 3" round cookie cutter.

CHEF BABA TIP: Any leftover dough can be rolled into 7 to 8 inch strips and formed into circles to make additional doughnuts.

5. Pour the canola oil in a 3" deep skillet so it is 2" deep. Heat the oil on medium-high until hot. The oil is ready when it begins to bubble. Drop a small piece of dough into the hot oil to test it—if the dough rises, the oil is ready.

6. Place 4 or 5 doughnuts at a time into the oil. Cover with a lid for the first 30 seconds to 1 minute of frying, then turn over and fry the other side, uncovered. Both sides will be golden brown. Remove the doughnuts with a large slotted spoon and place on a plate lined with paper towels to cool.

7. Sprinkle with powdered sugar and serve. You may also add a dollop of fruit preserves to the top.

In a large bowl, Damir combines the warm milk, egg yolks, sugar, salt and butter. Mixes with a wooden spoon until smooth.

In a separate bowl, Damir stirs together the flour, dry yeast and sugar, then adds it to the first bowl. Stirs 2 or 3 minutes until smooth—pulling dough toward him with the spoon as he turns the bowl.

Baba demonstrates how to make dough.

Chef Baba Tip: If the dough begins to stick to the bowl, sprinkle the sides of the bowl with a little flour as you mix.

Baba covers the bowl of dough with a cloth, then places a small pillow on top to keep the dough warm as it rises. She allows the dough to set for about 1 hour, or until the dough doubles in size.

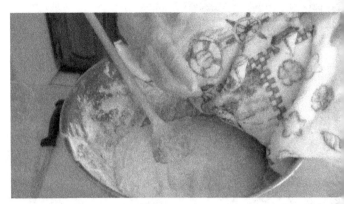

After the dough has risen, Baba generously sprinkles her work surface with all-purpose flour.

She lays the dough on the work surface, and sprinkles flour over it. Folds the dough in half once. Using a rolling pin, gently rolls the dough until it is about 1 finger thick.

Baba's granddaughter Danijela and Isabella Cooper cut the dough into circles using a 3" round cookie cutter. Any leftover dough can be rolled into 7 to 8 inch strips and formed into circles to make additional doughnuts.

In a 3" deep skillet, Baba pours the canola oil so it is 2" deep. Heats the oil on medium-high until hot. The oil is ready when it begins to bubble.

Baba places 4 or 5 doughnuts at a time into the oil. Covers with a lid for the first 30 seconds to 1 minute of frying, then turns it over to fry the other side, uncovered. Both sides will be golden brown.

Chef Baba

Kiflice with Apricot Filling

Serbian Crescent Cookies. These little crescent cookies have a delicate, flaky crust and are filled with apricot preserves. They are delicious warm or cold and can be kept for days or weeks in a closed container. No refrigeration is necessary.

- Season 3: Episode 2
- Preparation time: 2+ hours
- Cooking Time: 25 minutes
- Makes 60

Dough Ingredients:

9 ¾ cups all-purpose flour
2 packets dry yeast
3 eggs
1 handful granulated sugar
2 pinches of salt
2 cups whole milk
½ cup water
2 cups Crisco shortening
1 packet vanilla sugar
1 cup ground pecans

Instructions:

1. Place 8 cups of the flour in a large mixing bowl. Add the yeast and stir. Add the sugar, one whole egg and one egg yolk. Set the extra egg white aside for the filling (recipe below). Add the salt.

2. Heat the milk and add ½ cup water, then pour into the flour mixture. Stir the dough with a wooden spoon until smooth.

3. Flour your work surface. Place the dough on the surface, and flatten it with your hands forming a round layer about 1" thick.

4. Add the shortening, 1 ¼ cups of flour, one egg, and vanilla sugar in a medium mixing bowl. Mix with your hand until smooth.

5. Using a spatula, smooth the shortening mixture evenly over the layer of dough.

6. Fold the dough into thirds by first folding one side to the middle, then the other side to the middle. Then fold the other way into thirds by folding one end over the middle, then the other end over the middle to create a thick square of dough.

7. Cover the dough with a towel and a small pillow to hold in the warmth as the dough rises. Let it rest for 30 minutes.

8. After the dough has risen, remove the towel and pillow from the dough. Using a wooden rolling pin, gently roll out the dough. Roll from the middle toward the edges in all directions until the dough is about 1" thick. Fold the dough as you did before, into thirds and thirds again, to form a thick square. Cover again with a towel and pillow, and let it rise for another 30 minutes. Go and watch soccer while you wait. The dough will smell nice!

Kiflice with Apricot Filling   47

9. After 30 minutes, remove the towel and pillow. Gently roll the dough out, as before, to 1" thick. Fold into thirds, both ways, as before, to form a thick square. Cover and allow the dough to rise for another 30 minutes.

Make the Apricot Filling (recipe below) while you wait for the dough to rise.

1. Preheat the oven to 375 degrees.

2. Sprinkle the dough with a little flour. Using a wooden rolling pin, roll the dough out to about 1" thick. Cut into pieces about 3" square. Place ½ teaspoon of apricot filling in the middle of each square.

3. To form each Kiflice, fold one corner of the dough across the middle. Press the top of each Kiflice into a bowl of the remaining ground pecans. Place the Kiflice on a baking sheet about 1" apart.

4. Bake at 375 for 25 to 35 minutes or until golden brown. Remove from the oven, allow to cool. Enjoy warm or cool.

Apricot Pecan Filling Ingredients:

    1 jar (1 lb. 2 oz. or 510 grams)
       apricot preserves
    2 ½ cups ground pecans

1. Pour the apricot preserves into a small mixing bowl. Add the ground pecans, or enough to thicken the preserves. Mix well.

Puts 8 cups of flour in a bowl. Adds the yeast and stirs. Adds sugar. Adds one egg and one egg yolk. Adds the salt. Heats the milk and adds ½ c. water, then pours into the flour mixture.

Baba pours the ½ cup of flour into a separate bowl. She dips her hand and continues mixing the dough, holding the bowl in place with her other hand.

Baba teaches Damir to flour his work surface. He places the dough on the surface, and flattens it with his hands forming a round layer about 1" thick.

Baba uses a spatula to smooth the shortening mixture evenly over the layer of dough.

Damir folds the dough into thirds by first folding one side to the middle, then the other side to the middle. Then he folds the other way into thirds by folding one end over the middle, then the other end over the middle.

Baba covers the dough with a towel and a small pillow to hold in warmth as the dough rises. She lets it rest for 30 minutes.

Baba tells Jon Dylan, her grandson, about his dad and uncle eating everything in sight before she was finished making it. That includes Kiflice too.

Baba removes the towel and pillow from the dough. Using a wooden rolling pin, she gently rolls out the dough. She rolls from middle toward the edges in all directions until the dough is about 1" thick. She folds the dough as she did before, into thirds and thirds again, to form a thick square.

After covering again with a towel and pillow, and letting it rise for another 30 minutes, Damir removes the towel to show the layered dough. Baba preheats the oven to 375.

Kiflice with Apricot Filling   49

Chef Baba

Baba sprinkles the dough with a little flour. Using a wooden rolling pin she rolls the dough out to about 1" thick. Cuts into pieces about 3" square.

Baba places ½ teaspoon of apricot filling in the middle of each square. She folds each, folding one corner across to form a Kiflice.

Bakes at 375 for 25 minutes or until golden brown.

Baba removes Kiflice from the oven, she allows it to cool. She sprinkles powdered sugar over the Kiflice while Damir counts how many of them he is going to consume quickly.

The Three Strudels

Baba's Three Strudels—Poppy Seed, Pecan and Apricot. Baba makes all three kinds at one time so everyone in the family can enjoy their favorite.

- Season 2: Episode 3
- Preparation time: 35 min to 1 hour
- Baking Time: 35 minutes
- Serves 6-12 per strudel
  (Makes 3 strudels)

Strudel Dough Ingredients:

8 cups all-purpose flour
2 packets dry yeast
1 cup extra virgin olive oil
2 cups milk
1 handful (½ cup) granulated sugar
1 pinch salt
2 eggs
½ cups milk and ½ cup water

Dough Instructions:

1. Mix the flour and dry yeast in a medium bowl. Set aside. Heat the milk and put into a separate large mixing bowl. Add the olive oil, ½ cup sugar and salt. Mix with a fork.

2. Add the eggs, half of the flour and the yeast mixture. Stir with a wooden spoon, adding the hot milk and water mixture as needed. Add the remainder of the flour and yeast mixture. Stir until thoroughly mixed. The dough will be soft.

3. Place the dough on a floured work surface. Knead the dough, gently rolling into a ball. Knead until the dough is smooth and the ingredients are mixed thoroughly. Divide the dough into three equal parts. Knead each part again, until smooth and form into balls. Set two of the three dough balls aside.

4. Roll one ball of dough with a rolling pin, then pick it up and stretch it with your hands forming a rectangular shape about 12" x 8". Place the dough flat on the work surface.

Poppy Seed Strudel Filling Ingredients:

1 packet vanilla sugar
3 cups (1 pound) ground poppy
  seeds
1 handful (½ cup) granulated sugar
¼ cup milk

Poppy Seed Strudel Instructions:

1. Mix together the vanilla sugar, poppy seeds and ½ cup of granulated sugar in a medium bowl. Spread the poppy seed mixture evenly across the dough leaving a ½" to 1" margin of dough around the edges. Sprinkle the poppy seeds with milk to moisten them to make it easier to roll the strudel. Spray a 10" x 15" cookie sheet with cooking oil.

2. Carefully roll the strudel along the long side, rolling the dough away from you. Roll nearly all the way, then stop and pull the last flap of dough up toward you and over the top of the rolled dough. Place the rolled poppy seed strudel on the cookie sheet.

Pecan Strudel Filling Ingredients:

3 cups ground pecans
1 handful (½ cup) granulated sugar
1 packet vanilla sugar

Pecan Strudel Instructions:

1. Use a rolling pin to roll out the second ball of dough as described above. Mix together the ground pecans, sugar, and vanilla sugar. Spread the pecan mixture evenly over the dough.

2. Same as before, carefully roll the strudel along the long side, rolling the dough away from you. Roll nearly all the way, then stop and pull the last flap of dough up toward you, over the top of the rolled dough. Place the roll of Pecan Strudel on the cookie sheet alongside the first strudel roll.

Apricot Filling:

1 jar apricot preserves

Apricot Strudel Instructions:

1. Use a rolling pin to roll out the third ball of dough as described above. Add several dollops of apricot preserves over the stretched dough. Same as before,

carefully roll the strudel along the long side, rolling the dough away from you. Roll nearly all the way, then stop and pull the last flap of dough up toward you, over the top of the rolled dough. Place alongside the other two strudels.

2. Place a clean cloth over the three strudels. Wait one hour for the dough to rise.

3. Bake at 375 degrees for 35 minutes or until golden brown. Take the strudels off of the pan and place on a cooling rack, then cover with a cloth. Cool and serve.

In a medium bowl, Damir mixes the flour and dry yeast. Sets it aside.

The dough will be soft as shown.

Baba places the dough on a floured work surface. Kneads the dough. Divides the dough into three equal parts. Kneads each part again, until they are smooth and formed into balls.

Baba rolls one ball of dough with a rolling pin, and picks up and stretches it with her hands until the dough is a rectangular shape about 12" x 8".

She spreads the poppy seed mixture evenly across the dough.

She leaves a ½" to 1" margin of dough around the edges. Sprinkles the poppy seed layer with the ¼ cup milk to moisten the poppy seeds and roll easier.

Baba adds dollops of apricot preserves over the stretched dough.

She bakes at 375 for 35 minutes or until golden brown. Yummy.

The Three Strudels   55

Potato Biscuits

These hearty, old-world biscuits are enjoyed for any occasion. Simple to make, and easy to eat.

- Season 2: Episode 8
- Total Time to Make: 1 ½ hours
- Makes about 32

Ingredients:

7 large potatoes
1 pinch of salt
1 tablespoon olive oil
2 eggs
All-purpose flour (enough to make ⅓ ratio to ⅔ potatoes)
2 teaspoons baking soda

Instructions:

1. Place the whole potatoes, leaving on the skins, in a large pot. Cover completely with water. Cover with a lid and heat over high until boiling. Boil for about 4 minutes, or until the potatoes are tender when poked with a fork.

2. Remove the potatoes from heat. Strain off the water. Allow the potatoes to cool about 5 minutes. While the potatoes are still hot, carefully remove the skins by holding a potato in one hand, using a folded paper towel to keep from burning your hand. With your other hand, use a knife to peel the potato skin off in strips.

3. Place the potatoes in a large mixing bowl. Allow to cool.

4. Mash the potatoes with a potato masher. Mix in the salt, olive oil and eggs.

5. Add enough flour to make a 1/3 ratio of flour to 2/3 of potatoes. Add the baking soda and mix the dough with your hands.

6. Lightly flour your work surface. Knead the dough until smooth. Add a little flour to the surface as needed to keep the dough from sticking.

7. Flatten the dough with your hands to about 1" thick. Cut into circles using a biscuit cutter: either 1 ½" for appetizers or 2" for full biscuits.

8. Spray a large cookie sheet with cooking oil. Place the biscuits about 1" apart on the sheet. Bake at 375 degrees for 20 minutes. Turn the biscuits over and bake a few minutes longer. They should be golden brown. Remove from the oven and enjoy!

Baba places the whole potatoes, leaving the skins, in a large pot. Adds water. Covers with lid and heats over high heat until boiling. Boils for about 4 minutes.

Baba teaches Danijela to mash the potatoes with a potato masher while Damir ponders how to make the process more automated. That is so Damir.

Baba works the dough.

Baba lightly adds flour to her work surface. Places the dough on the surface and kneads until smooth. Adds a little flour to the surface as needed to keep the dough from sticking.

Baba flattens the dough to about 1 finger thick. Cuts it into circles using a biscuit cutter: either 1 ½" for appetizers or 2" for full biscuits.

Baba bakes the biscuits at 375 degrees for 20 minutes. She turns biscuits over and bakes a few minutes more. The biscuits should be golden brown.

Perfect for eating at any time.

Baba sprays a large cookie sheet with cooking oil. Places the biscuits about 1" apart on the sheet.

Soups and Salads

The reason for starting the Chef Baba's Cooking Show and developing the Chef Baba's Cookbook was that my son Damir wanted to preserve the tradition of making my Famous Chicken Noodle Soup. He believes my soup has magical properties. My Magic Green Salad has helped me lose sixty pounds in less than twelve months. The soups and salads have helped me develop a healthy plan to lose weight and keep my weight down. At 85 years old, I feel healthier than ever.

Thanksgiving dinner at Chef Baba's with friends and family. Chef Baba's Chicken Noodle Soup is obviously the opening dish to the huge feast.

For Thanksgiving, I always make a huge meal. Ever since we came to America in 1974, we have celebrated this important American holiday with family and extended family.

In the early years, our family members from Austin, Texas drove up for Thanksgiving dinner. There must have been 30 to 40 people at the long dinner table that extended from one room into the next.

Chicken noodle soup is one of the dishes I am known for in my large family. Whenever my children or grandchildren are sick, I make it. It helps them recover quickly. Of the entire family, there is no bigger fan of the soup than Damir. He

loves sipping the soup when it is still piping hot.

One Thanksgiving, I was under time pressure to prepare the feast and ran out of Vegeta, as well as my famous noodles. I was forced to use salt and pepper, rather than Vegeta, and store-bought noodles.

As usual, Damir dished out the soup for everyone at the table. After serving at least 15 people, he finally placed enough noodles and soup into his own bowl. He sat down and prepared to devour it. And then he put his head down to smell it. (Damir has an incredibly sensitive sense of smell.)

"Baba, you cheated," he said smiling. I smiled without saying a word.

"You cheated, Baba. This is not your soup," he repeated, wagging his finger at me. He pushed the soup away from him.

One of the guests asked, "It is an awesome soup. You're not going to eat it?"

"No," he replied.

"Damire, you are right. I ran out of ingredients. You don't have to eat it," I said.

I could tell some of the guests thought Damir was extremely rude to me. But that is the Serbian way. Being direct.

Damir refused to compromise on his principles of tasting perfection. He knew my soup by the smell. He has tasted it thousands of times. He knows its perfection and would not settle for less. It is one of the highest compliments I

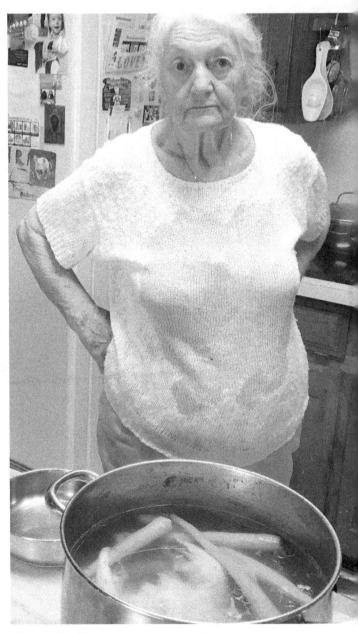

"In my life, I have never met a pickier and more eccentric person than Damir. I don't know how he became that way. Sometimes I think he is not my son. For a cooking imbecile, he sure demands perfection when I cook. He will not settle for anything other than how I make it traditionally. I guess I have spoiled him, and that is my fault. He believes that I am the best chef in the world."

have ever received as a cook over the last seventy-five years. It may not have shown on my face, but my heart was filled with joy that Thanksgiving night. I was thankful that my family appreciated my cooking.

If you cook for your family as much as I have over the years, this kind of compliment is something every cook cherishes.

Damir cleaned up all of the dishes that night (he always does it), but not once did he come close to tasting my modified soup.

—Love, Chef Baba

Baba's Famous Chicken Noodle Soup

This is the soup that Baba's family enjoys at every holiday and throughout the winter. They say it has magical healing properties and is the best soup in the world. Damir will only eat it if it has Baba's homemade noodles.

- Season 1: Episode 5
- Preparation time: 15 minutes
- Cooking Time: 3 hours
- Serves 10-12

Chicken Broth Ingredients:

1 yellow onion
1 whole raw chicken, about 3 ½ pounds
3 parsnips
6 large whole carrots
1 heaping tablespoon Vegeta (or soup starter)
1 pinch of salt (about 2 teaspoons)

Instructions:

1. Cut the onion in half and grill on the stove by placing both onion halves, cut side down, onto a stove-top burner set to medium heat. Remove when the onion is golden brown.

2. Wash the chicken very well. Cut off any excess fat. Place the entire chicken in a large, deep pot, and cover with cold water. Add the onion halves to the pot.

3. Peel the parsnips with a vegetable peeler. Cut off the ends, cut in half, length-wise, then add to the pot. Peel the carrots, cut off the ends and add to the pot.

4. Cover the pot and bring the soup to a boil over high heat. Using a large spoon, skim off any foamy fat from the surface, as it appears, and discard.

5. Turn the heat down to medium and boil the soup gently for 2 to 3 hours, skimming off the fat as needed so that the soup will be clear.

6. After 1 hour, add the vegeta. Reduce the heat to low, and simmer for 1 hour more. Add a pinch of salt to taste. Simmer for another 30 minutes, until the onion is tender and the chicken is done.

7. Strain the broth through a wire strainer and into another large pot.

8. Add Baba's homemade noodles just before serving (see separate recipe) to the chicken broth. Add the cooked carrots and parsnips to the soup or offer them on the side. Serve the soup piping hot.

CHEF BABA TIP: Use the cooked chicken to make Baba's Russian Chicken Salad (see separate recipe).

Damir tells Baba that he didn't know she grilled the onion on the stove when she was making the soup. "You never asked," said Baba.

Baba shows how the onion should look.

Damir discusses with Baba the art of making Baba's Famous Chicken Noodle Soup.

Baba washes the chicken very well. Cuts off any excess fat. Places the entire chicken in a large, deep pot, and covers with cold water. Adds the onion halves to the pot.

She peels the parsnips with a vegetable peeler. Cuts off the ends, cuts in half, length-wise, then adds to the pot.

Baba peels the carrots, cuts off the ends and adds to the pot.

Baba covers the pot and brings the soup to a boil over high heat. Using a spoon, skims off any foamy fat from the surface, as it appears, and discards.

Baba boils the soup gently for 2 to 3 hours, skimming off the fat as needed so that the soup will be clear.

Just before serving, Baba adds her homemade noodles (see separate recipe) to the chicken broth.

Baba's daughter Jelena serves soup for each guest.

Baba's Famous Chicken Noodle Soup   67

When we began filming the Chef Baba Cooking Show, I knew that one recipe we had to do was Baba's Super-Thin Noodles. Whenever I eat Baba's Famous Chicken Noodle Soup, I think of the famous line from Jerry Maguirre, "You had me at hello." And that is exactly how I feel about Baba's noodles every time I sip her soup. If you've watched our show, you know I love the soup to be super hot.

"Baba, you had me at *noodles*," I think as I sip the extremely hot chicken broth and slurp those super-long, super-thin noodles. I refuse to eat her soup without her homemade noodles. I started the show as a cooking imbecile but after so many seasons and episodes, I am gaining the confidence to cook. But making these noodles intimidates me. Of all of the Chef Baba recipes, her noodles and Reforma Torta are the most intimidating for me to make.

I have eaten in a lot of good Italian restaurants. I have been to Rome a few times and eaten some great Italian dishes with noodles. But I have never tasted better noodles than Chef Baba's Super-Thin Noodles. I hope one day to be able to make them just like Chef Baba.

One amazing thing about her noodles is that you can make them and store them for several months. And they will stay delicious.

—Love, Damir
"Chef Baba's Sous Chef"

Baba's Super-Thin Noodles

These are the only noodles Baba will allow in her homemade chicken noodle soup. They are a simple recipe with only two ingredients, however they are a bit complicated to make. They are certainly worth the extra effort.

- Season 1: Episode 6
- Preparation time: 35 to 40 minutes
- Serves 10-12

Ingredients:

4 eggs
2 cups all-purpose flour

Instructions:

1. Break the eggs into a medium mixing bowl and mix slightly with a fork. Add the flour. Mix together with one hand until smooth, holding the bowl in place with your other hand. Scrape off excess dough from your hand as necessary, using a butter knife. Continue mixing.

2. Form the dough into a ball and place on a floured surface. Knead the dough, rolling it with the palms of your hands. Sprinkle a little additional flour onto the surface as the dough begins to stick. Knead until smooth, then form into a ball.

3. Using a rolling pin, roll the dough from the middle outward, toward the edges. Turn the dough 90 degrees, frequently at first, so it is rolled in all directions. Roll gently until the dough is about 1/8" to ¼' thick.

4. Cut the dough into strips to fit through your noodle machine. Feed each strip through the noodle machine twice to make it paper-thin. Carefully lay the long strips of dough on a table or counter covered with a cloth, so they do not touch. Turn the dough strips over, as needed to prevent the dough from drying out.

5. While the dough strips are still slightly moist, feed each strip through the noodle machine to make very thin noodles. Place the noodles in a pile, on a clean cloth. Leave them to dry overnight. Either store the dry noodles in a box, layered between paper towels to protect them from breaking; or add to hot soup and enjoy. Drop the dry noodles into the hot soup for 3 minutes and they will be ready to eat.

Breaks the eggs into a medium mixing bowl and mixes slightly with a fork.

Adds the flour.

Mixes together with one hand until smooth, holding the bowl in place with her other hand. Scrapes off excess dough from her hand as necessary, using a butter knife.

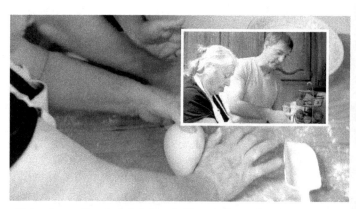

Baba forms the dough into a ball and places it on a floured surface. Kneads the dough, rolling it with the palms of her hands.

Using a rolling pin, she rolls the dough from the middle outward, toward the edges.

Turns the dough 90 degrees, frequently at first, so it is rolled in all directions.

Baba explains to Damir with joy the art of making noodles.

Rolls gently until the dough is about ⅛" to ¼' thick.

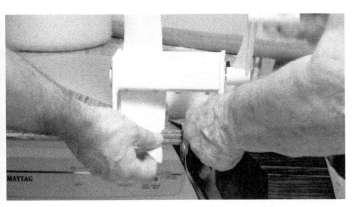

Baba cuts the dough into strips to fit through her noodle machine. Damir feeds each strip through the noodle machine twice to make it paper-thin.

Baba lays the strips of dough on a table or counter covered with a cloth, so they do not touch. Turns the dough strips over, as needed to prevent the dough from drying out.

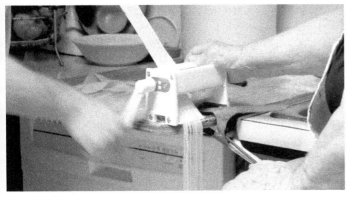

While the dough strips are still slightly moist, Damir feeds each strip through the noodle machine to make very thin noodles.

Baba places the noodles in a pile, on a clean cloth. Leaves them to dry overnight.

Growing up in Yugoslavia, whenever I saw Chef Baba making her famous Chicken Noodle Soup, I understood the process even at an early age. It was simple.

When Baba makes the soup, she makes her super thin noodles (unless she made some a few months earlier and had stored them in a box for the future) and then she uses the remaining chicken to make Russian Chicken Salad. It was a classic case of Pavlov's conditioning: Soup always leads to Russian salad.

For many years I did not know why it was called Russian Chicken Salad. I guess I was too busy devouring this incredible salad to think about the origin of the name. I mean, why not call it Serbian, Croatian, Bosnian or any of the other former Yugoslavian republics' salad?

Being an astute critic of Chef Baba's food through years of enjoying her dishes, my job was to devour them—not to make them or think about them.

But I finally discovered the story behind the name of the Russian Chicken Salad. In Russia, the salad was originally called Olivier Salad. The original version of the salad was concocted in 1860s by Lucien Olivier, the chef at the Hermitage restaurant in Moscow.

Originally, it was made from lettuce, caviar, smoked duck, capers, hazel grouse, and other delicacies.

The second version of the salad was made from boiled and diced potatoes and carrots, diced Bologna sausage and pickled cucumbers. This version of Olivier salad was extremely popular in the Soviet Union, and is still popular in Russia. The recipe was kept secret until Chef Olivier's sous chef stole the recipe and popularized it through his own restaurant, cooking magazines and books.

Russians don't put the salad on bread. However, I enjoy this wonderful salad as a side dish with various main dishes from pork to beef, and I eat it as a meal in itself. One of my favorite ways to eat it is on a sandwich with smoked Serbian sausage like the kind my father used to make when we lived on the farm.

One thing that makes Russian Salad so delicious is a small thing you might overlook—the pickles. They deliver just the right amount of sour flavor to make the dish interesting. Can you tell I've eaten it a few times?

—Love, Damir

"Chef Baba's Sous Chef"

Russian Chicken Salad

In Russia, the salad was originally called Olivier Salad. But in my family, they didn't care what it was called—they were too busy eating it.

- Season 1: Episode 7
- Preparation time: 35 to 40 minutes
- Serves 10-12

Ingredients:

> 5 hard-boiled eggs
> Dash of salt
> Whole, cooked chicken (from
>   Baba's Chicken Soup Recipe)
> 3 or 4 cooked parsnips (from
>   Baba's Chicken Soup)
> Cooked carrots
> 5 or 6 medium, whole dill pickles
> Pinch of salt (~1 ½ teaspoon)
> Mayonnaise (Baba uses
>   Hellman's Mayonnaise)

Russian Salad and red wine, preferably a blend are an unusual way for Damir to enjoy both.

CHEF BABA'S TIP: Prepare this recipe using the chicken and vegetables from Baba's Famous Chicken Noodle Soup.

Instructions:

1. Finely chop the parsnips and carrots, by cutting them in thirds lengthwise, then chopping into 1/4-inch pieces. Place them in a large bowl.

2. Remove the bones, skin and any fat from the chicken and place the meat on a cutting board.

3. Chop the chicken into 1/2 inch pieces with a large knife, then add to the carrots and parsnips. Chop the eggs into ¼" cubes and add to the bowl.

4. Stir the mixture with a fork, adding mayonnaise to taste.

5. Refrigerate overnight and serve.

There is no delicious Russian Chicken Salad without Baba first making her Famous Chicken Soup.

The Russian Salad is a derivative of her incredible, magical, unbelievable soup.

Baba separates the chicken broth from the rest of the ingredients. Part of those ingredients are used for her Russian Salad.

Baba finely chops the parsnips and carrots, by cutting them in thirds lengthwise, then chopping into ¼" pieces. Places them in a large bowl.

Baba chops the chicken into ½" pieces with a large knife, then adds it to the carrots and parsnips. She chops the eggs into ¼" cubes and adds them to the bowl.

Damir's plate the day after Thanksgiving. He had eaten too much turkey and chose to eat lighter. Shown is roasted bell peppers, tomato salad, sweet mashed potatoes and Russian Salad.

Russian Chicken Salad   75

Damir discusses knives with Baba. He's preparing
to sharpen them for the job.

When I was a kid in Yugoslavia, we often ate Pasulj for lunch or late dinner. I don't know how I got the impression that Pasulj was a dish only poor people ate. Maybe because our neighbor made it so often for her family. She watched us when both of my parents were working, and it seemed like she made Pasulj just about every day. I ate it heartily and thought she made it often to save money.

Today I look at Pasulj with great pride, understanding and respect. I eat it as much as I can because it is nutritious. I love all kinds of bean dishes. Of course, I am extremely picky about the type of bean dishes I like to eat. I prefer them to be thick.

Chef Baba lost a substantial amount of weight eating her Baba's Magic Salad and Pasulj. If you want to know how much, check out her Baba's Magic Salad recipe. You will be inspired to eat more salad and Pasulj.

—Love, Damir
"Chef Baba's Sous Chef"

Serbian Cooked Beans

Pasulj, a true Serbian classic. This is a hearty comfort food and simple to prepare.

- Season 4: Episode 3
- Total Time to Make: 2 hours
  (+ over night if using dried beans)
- Serves: 8

Ingredients:

1 large white onion
1 (1 pound) bag of dry pinto beans, kidney beans or black beans (or 2 cans of beans)
2 tablespoons coconut oil, olive oil or other cooking oil. (Baba likes Luann's Coconut Oil)
1 teaspoon Vegeta
1 ½ cup water
1 yellow bell pepper, cut into four pieces
6 tablespoons olive oil
6 tablespoons all-purpose flour

CHEF BABA TIP: To prepare dried beans, rinse and then cover with cold water. Allow to soak overnight. Drain off the water. Cover the beans with cold water and bring to a boil for 5 minutes. Drain off the water. Cover the beans with warm water and boil a second time for 5 minutes. Drain off the water. Boil a third time for 5 minutes, drain and allow to cool.

Instructions:

1. Chop the onion and place in a large skillet with 2 tablespoons of cooking oil. Cover and heat over medium-low until the onions are tender. Stir occasionally. When the onions become translucent, increase the heat to medium-high and continue cooking. Sprinkle Vegeta over the onions, cover and continue cooking until the onions are light brown.

2. Add the beans and water to the onions. Stir, cover and lower the heat to medium. Add the yellow bell pepper.

3. Prepare a zaprazhka (or roux) to thicken the beans. In a small skillet, heat the olive oil over medium high. Add the flour, stirring until smooth. Continue cooking, stirring frequently until thick and light brown.

4. Add the zaprazhka (or roux) to the beans. Stir the beans gently and continue cooking until thickened. You can enjoy them thick or add water to make them a soup. Remove from heat and enjoy.

Baba chops the onion. Places it in a large skillet, adds the cooking oil.

Baba heats the onions over medium-low until they are tender.

Baba prepares a zaprazhka (or roux) to thicken the beans.

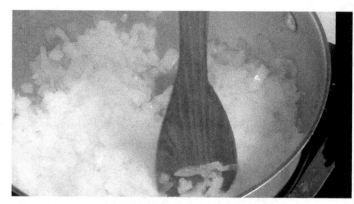

She stirs occasionally. When the onions become translucent, Baba increases the heat to medium-high and continues cooking.

She adds the beans to the onions and water. Stirs, covers and lowers the heat to medium.

Baba adds the yellow bell pepper.

In the meantime, Baba prepares zaprazhka to thicken the beans. In a small skillet, heats the olive oil over medium-high. Adds the flour, stirring until smooth.

Continues cooking, stirring frequently until thick and light brown. Adds the zaprazhka to the beans.

Baba stirs the beans gently and continues cooking until thickened. (You can enjoy it thick or add water to make it a soup. Remove from heat and enjoy.)

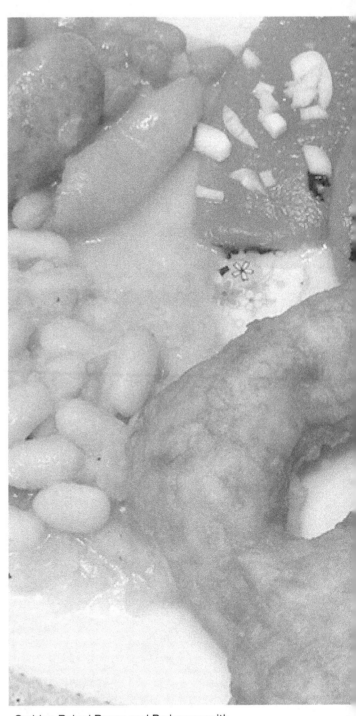

Serbian Baked Beans and Prebranac with Lepinjice and sausage.

Serbian Cooked Beans   79

Prebranac (Serbian Baked Beans)

Chef Baba serves this every Christmas Eve. These delicious baked beans are simple to make.

- Season 4: Episode 3
- Preparation Time: 20-30 minutes
  (+ over night if using dried beans)
- Cooking Time: 30 minutes
- Serves: 8

Ingredients:

2 large white onion
1 bag (1 lb.) of dry cannellini beans, peruano beans or white kidney beans (or use canned beans)
2 tablespoons coconut oil (olive oil or other cooking oil. Baba likes Luann's Coconut Oil)
2 teaspoons Vegeta
1 tablespoon olive oil
1 teaspoon black pepper
1 teaspoon ground red pepper (optional)
1 ½ cup hot water

CHEF BABA TIP: To prepare dried beans, rinse and then cover with cold water. Allow to soak overnight. Drain off the water. Cover the beans with cold water and bring to boil for 5 minutes. Drain off the water. Cover the beans with warm water and boil a second time for 5 minutes. Drain off the water. Boil a third time for 5 minutes, drain and allow to cool.

Instructions:

1. Preheat the oven to 350 degrees.

2. Chop the onion and place in a large skillet with 2 tablespoons of cooking oil and sauté the onions. Cover and heat over medium-low until the onions are tender. Stir occasionally. When onions become translucent, increase the heat to medium-high and continue cooking. Sprinkle 1 teaspoon of the Vegeta on top, cover and continue cooking until the onions are light brown. Remove from heat.

3. Spread olive oil across the bottom of a large, deep baking dish. Spoon half of the beans into the dish in an even layer. Add all of the onions in an even layer over the beans. Spoon the remaining beans over the onions. Season with a little vegeta, black pepper and red pepper. Pour the hot water over the top of the beans.

4. Bake at 350 for 30 minutes.

Baba chops the onion.

She sautés the onions. Covers and heats over medium-low until the onions are tender.

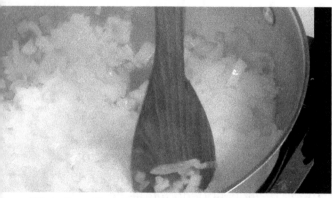

When the onions become translucent, Baba increases the heat to medium-high and continues cooking. Sprinkles Vegeta on top, covers and continues cooking until the onions are light brown.

Baba teaches Damir the art of waiting during the cooking process.

Baba spoons half of the beans into the dish in an even layer. Adds all of the onions in an even layer over the beans. Spoons the remaining beans over the onions.

Seasons with a little Vegeta, black pepper and red pepper. Pours the hot water over the top of the beans.

Bakes at 350 for 30 minutes.

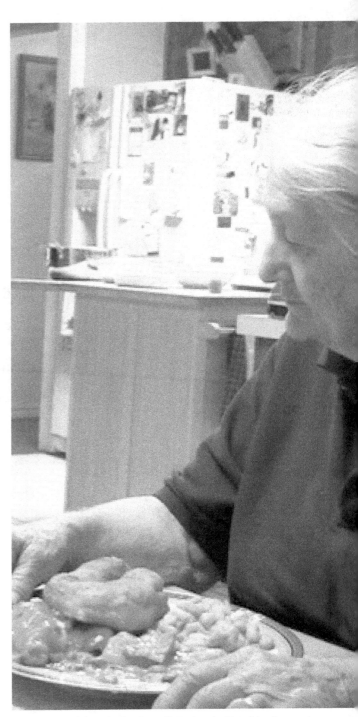

Baba and Damir taste the Prebranac. Every Christmas, Chef Baba has made it for the family.

Damir discusses American politics with Baba while eating Prebranac and Lepinjice.

Baba gets a headache from listening to Damir's discussion on American politics.

Prebranac (Serbian Baked Beans)   83

Before: Chef Baba (2014)

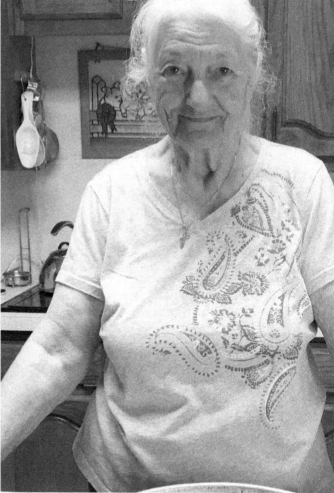

Now: Chef Baba (2017)

You are never too old to lose weight. There is no excuse. You can do it if you (1) set your mind to it, (2) plan on losing weight over a longer period of time, and (3) change your diet.

At 82 years old, I weighed 239 pounds. I had been on the heavier side for about forty years. When I was younger living in Yugoslavia, I was much thinner. Unfortunately, I gained all my weight living in America.

It is never too late to start eating right. I developed my own healthy eating plan that helped me lose 80 pounds. This wonderful salad was a large part of my plan. I ate three meals a day. I ate meat only twice a week, avoided bread and supplemented my protein needs by eating beans. I enjoyed all kinds of bean dishes.

Losing weight is not a get rich quick scheme. It requires discipline. It is important to lose it slowly but consistently. I lost 60 pounds over the first twelve months, and an additional 20 pounds over the following year. Today I am 160 pounds. Many people lose weight and then gain it back. I have remained at my current weight for the last two years.

Look at me before and now.

—Love, Chef Baba

Baba's Magic Salad

This scrumptious salad can be eaten on any occasion.

- Season 3: Episode 6
- Preparation Time: 20 to 30 minutes
- Serves: 4 to 6

Ingredients:

1 (5-oz) bag of spring mix lettuce
1 large leek
2 or 3 carrots, diced
1 red bell pepper, sliced into ¼"
pieces
1 avocado, halved and cut into
¼" slices
½ red onion, thinly sliced and
halved
1 head bok choy, leaves and
stems, sliced into ¼" pieces
1 pinch salt
1 or 2 tablespoons grapeseed oil
1 or 2 tablespoons white
wine vinegar
1 heaping teaspoon flax seeds
1 handful sunflower seeds
(or chopped pecans or walnuts,
or pumpkin seeds)
1 tablespoon raspberry salad
dressing (Baba likes Ken's
Salad Dressings)

Instructions:

1. Remove any spoiled leaves from the spring mix, place in a large mixing bowl.

Damir proudly displays the simplicity, beauty and the magic of Baba's Magic Salad.

2. Slice the leek in half lengthwise, then chop in ¼" pieces, and add to the lettuce. Add the carrots, bell pepper, avocado, and bok choy.

3. Mix all together gently so you don't smash the avocado.

4. Dress the salad by adding the salt, grapeseed oil, flax seeds and raspberry dressing.

5. Toss gently until the dressing is evenly distributed.

6. Taste and adjust seasonings as desired.

Damir is impressed with Baba's attention to detail. She shows him how to remove any spoiled leaves from spring mix.

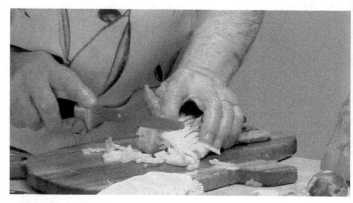

Baba slices the leek in half lengthwise, then chops it in ¼" pieces, and adds to the lettuce.

Damir adds the carrots, bell pepper, avocado, and bok choy to the salad bowl.

Baba cuts the onions for the salad.

Baba loves onions in the salad. Damir prefers to leave them out. You chose whether to add or not.

When you mix it all together, make sure that you do it gently so you don't smash the avocado.

Baba adds the salt, grapeseed oil, flax seeds and raspberry dressing to the salad.

Baba teaches Damir to toss the salad gently until the dressing is distributed because she knows he has a ruffian personality at times. Not always, but most of the time.

Taste and adjust seasonings as desired. Enjoy.

Baba's Magic Salad is nutritious and beautiful to display because of all the contrasting colors.

Baba's Magic Salad   87

Kisela Čorba

Kisela Čorba (Sour Chicken Soup). This special Serbian soup beautifully blends the flavors of chicken and lemon. A great soup for summer.

- Season 5
- Preparation Time: 3 hours
- Cooking Time: 30 minutes
- Serves: 8

Ingredients:

1 whole, raw chicken
2 large parsnips, peeled and cut
  in half lengthwise
5 large carrots, peeled
½ yellow onion
1 tablespoon salt
1 tablespoon peppercorns
1 tablespoon Vegeta
3 tablespoons vegetable oil
6 heaping tablespoons
  all-purpose flour
1 ¼ cup water
⅔ cup plain yogurt
1 egg yolk
1 teaspoon ground pepper
Juice of one lemon

Instructions:

1. Wash the chicken and place in a large pot with water. Add the parsnips, carrots and the entire half onion. Fill with water about 2" above the chicken.

2. Bring to a boil over high heat, then reduce to low. Add the salt and peppercorns, and simmer for 2 hours. Using a large spoon, skim off the foam as it appears on the surface of the broth, and discard.

3. After one hour add the Vegeta and continue cooking for the last hour. Remove the soup from the heat. Remove the chicken and the vegetables from the chicken broth. Set aside.

4. Prepare a zaprazhka (or roux) by mixing the vegetable oil and 2 tablespoons of flour in a medium skillet. Heat over medium-high, stirring frequently until smooth and brown. About 10 minutes.

5. Add at least two cups of chicken broth to the zaprazhka. Stir until smooth, then pour into a large pot.

6. Slowly mix the remaining the chicken broth into the zaprazhka, pouring the broth through a strainer to remove any vegetable pieces or chicken bits.

7. Mix 1 ¼ cup water, yogurt, 2 heaping tablespoons of flour and the egg yolk in a sauce pan. Bring to a boil over medium high. Boil for 2 minutes stirring constantly, until thick.

8. Add the ground pepper. Slowly stir the sauce into the soup. Add lemon juice and mix. Taste and adjust seasoning.

9. Add bite-sized pieces of chicken and vegetables, as desired, to the soup. Serve hot.

Baba washes the chicken and places it in a large pot with water. Adds the parsnips, carrots and the entire half onion. Fills it with water to 2" above the chicken.

She brings it to boil over high heat, then reduces to low. Adds the salt and peppercorns, and simmers for 2 hours. Skims off the foam as it forms on the surface of the broth, and discards.

After one hour, she adds vegeta and continues cooking for the last hour. Removes the soup from the heat. Removes the chicken and vegetables from the broth.

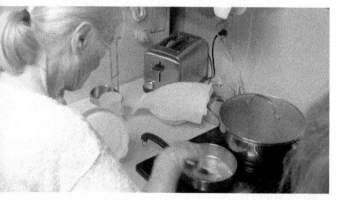

In a medium skillet, Baba makes a zaprazhka (or roux) by mixing the vegetable oil and 2 tablespoons of flour. Heats over medium-high, stirring frequently until smooth and brown. About 10 minutes.

Adds at least 2 cups of chicken broth to the zaprazhka. Stirs until smooth, then mixes it into the chicken broth. Slowly mixes the chicken broth into it, pouring the broth through a strainer to remove any vegetable or chicken bit.

In a saucepan, she mixes 1 ¼ cup water, yogurt, 2 heaping tablespoons of flour and the egg yolk. Brings it to a boil over medium high. Boils for 2 minutes stirring constantly, until thick.

Baba adds the ground pepper. Slowly stirs the sauce into the soup. Adds lemon juice and mixes. Tastes and adjusts the seasoning.

Baba adds bite-sized pieces of chicken and vegetables, as desired, to the soup. Serves hot.

Kisela Čorba   91

Baba's Tomato Salad

A simple, delicious celebration of fresh tomatoes.

- Season 5
- Preparation Time: 10-15 minutes
- Serves: 4 to 6

Ingredients:

> 2 large tomatoes, sliced thick
> 1 small white onion, diced
> ¼ cup white or red wine vinegar
> ⅓ cup grapeseed oil or olive oil
> ⅓ cup blue cheese, feta or Greek
>   cheese (crumbled)
> Salt and pepper to taste

Instructions:

1. Layer half of the tomatoes on the bottom of a serving dish. Sprinkle half of the onion over the tomatoes. Pour half of the oil and white vinegar of the tomatoes.

2. Place the remaining tomatoes over the first layer. Add the remaining onion, oil and vinegar.

3. Sprinkle cheese over the top. Cover and refrigerate for at least two hours before serving.

Baba prepares the ingredients.

The ingredients are simple.

Baba slices the tomatoes perfectly.

Baba sprinkles with salt and 2 chopped garlic cloves.

Baba pours the olive oil.

She adds cheese.

Baba's Cucumber Salad

Baba makes this cucumber salad often in the summer. It is refreshing to your palate.

- Season 5
- Preparation Time: 10 to 15 minutes
- Serves: 4 to 6

Ingredients:

1 large English cucumber
⅓ cup white vinegar
⅓ water
⅓ cup grapeseed, sunflower oil
   or olive oil
Salt and pepper to taste

Instructions:

1. Slice the cucumber. Mix the vinegar and water. Pour the mixture on top of the sliced cucumber.

2. Add the oil, plus salt and pepper to taste.

3. Mix thoroughly. Serve right away.

A perfect complement to any meal.

Baba's Potato Salad

Krompir Salad in Serbian. This very simple potato salad is one of the best you will ever taste.

- Season 5
- Preparation Time: 10 minutes
- Cooking Time: 8 to 15 minutes
- Serves: 4

Ingredients:

4 potatoes (white or russet)
1 teaspoon salt
⅓ cup vegetable oil
¼ onion (red or yellow onion)
2 to 3 tablespoons white vinegar

Ingredients:

1. Wash the whole potatoes and place them in a deep pan. Cover with water, add salt and bring to a boil. Continue boiling until the potatoes are just tender when poked with a fork. Do not over-cook.

2. Drain the water from the potatoes. While they are still hot, remove the skins.

CHEF BABA TIP: Hold each potato in your hand, using a folded paper towel to protect your fingers from the heat. Carefully use a paring knife to peel off the skin in strips.

Potato salad with roasted red peppers and fried catfish is heavenly.

3. Dice the potatoes and add vegetable oil (while the potatoes are still hot). Finely chop the onion and add to the potatoes, add white vinegar to taste. Gently mix together.

4. Serve this potato salad warm. Refrigerate any leftovers and enjoy it cold for two more days.

Baba's Cabbage Salad

This is healthy and simple to make. A tasty cabbage salad with a light dressing.

- Season 5
- Preparation Time: 10 to 15 minutes
- Serves: 4

Ingredients:

1 whole white cabbage
1 teaspoon sugar
½ teaspoon salt
⅓ cup safflower oil (sunflower or
  grapeseed oil)
⅓ white vinegar
Dash of black pepper

Instructions:

1. Thinly slice the cabbage. Place it in a large mixing bowl. Add the sugar and mix.

2. Let the salad set for 2 minutes.

3. Add the salt, vegetable oil, white vinegar and black pepper to taste.

A beautiful cabbage makes a great cabbage salad.

Baba cuts the cabbage. Slices it into thin layers.

Baba adds sugar, salt, vegetable oil and white vinegar.

Baba adds black pepper to taste. Jana is the official cabbage salad taster.

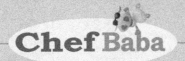

Main Courses

The heart and soul of Chef Baba's cooking traditions. You will go back thousands of years in food culture with Sarma, and you will feel like royalty when eating King Karadjordje's Schnitzel.

Oh no. I am going to speak Balkan blasphemy: I don't like Sarma. I didn't like Sarma as a kid growing up in Yugoslavia. I tried to like it. I really tried.

You know I can be difficult to please, if you have watched any of the Chef Baba Cooking shows. I'm sure you have heard Chef Baba say more than once, "Damire, you are so, so picky ... on everything."

I thought my taste buds would change as I grew older and that I would fall in love with Sarma—Not!

I don't know why I don't like it. Sarma is one of the most traditional Balkan recipes you can find. This dish is popular across the former Ottoman empire, from the Middle East to the Balkans and Central Europe. There are several variations of Sarma—depending on the culture and region of Ottoman influence throughout the centuries.

I never met another person in former Yugoslavia who did not love Sarma. And I never met an American who, upon tasting Chef Baba's Sarma, did not love it. So please ignore my taste buds.

Chef Baba loves Sarma, and she makes the best version of it. How do I know, if I don't like it? I see the joy in people's eyes. I see their smiles when they taste her Sarma.

So ... enjoy. May Sarma be with you in spirit, soul, heart and stomach.

—Love, Damir

"Chef Baba's Sous Chef"

Sarma

Stuffed cabbage. This is one of the most famous traditional dishes from Eastern Europe. It is cabbage leaves stuffed with seasoned beef or other ground meat.

- Season 3: Episode 1
- Total Time to Make: 2 hours
- Makes about 16 Cabbage Rolls

Ingredients:

> ¼ large yellow onion
> 1 tablespoon vegetable oil (Baba uses safflower oil)
> 2 pounds ground beef, chicken or pork
> 1 teaspoon salt
> ½ teaspoon pepper
> 1 teaspoon Vegeta
> 1 tablespoon paprika
> 2 large cabbages
> 2 tablespoons + 2 teaspoons white vinegar
> 2 eggs
> 2 handfuls white rice (uncooked)

Instructions:

1. Dice the onion, and place in large pot with the vegetable oil. Sauté over medium heat until the onion begins to brown. Add the ground meat and mix. Continue cooking over high heat. Stir as needed to cook evenly.

2. Adjust the temperature as needed. Season with salt, pepper and Vegeta to taste. The meat will be done in about 35 minutes.

3. Add the paprika after the meat is done. Taste it to see if you want to adjust the seasoning. Set aside while you prepare the cabbage.

4. To prepare the cabbage, fill a large pot half full of water. Bring the water to a boil. Cut the bottom core of the cabbage and discard. Also remove 2 or 3 of the outside leaves and discard.

5. When the water begins to boil, add 2 tablespoons of white vinegar. Place the whole cabbage in the boiling water. Using tongs, remove the outer leaves, one at a time, as they loosen and become soft. Stack the leaves on a plate to cool.

6. Drain the excess juice from the meat and pour into a large measuring cup. Add water to make 4 cups of liquid. Add 2 teaspoons of white vinegar. Stir and set aside.

7. Add the egg and uncooked white rice to the meat stuffing. Stir nicely.

To make a cabbage roll:

1. Cut off and discard the thick stem piece from the cabbage leaf.

2. Hold the cabbage leaf in the palm of one hand with the thick part of the leaf to the outside.

3. Put 2 heaping tablespoons of meat in the center of the cabbage. Shape the meat into a rectangle with a narrow end toward the outside, about 1" down from the thick part of the leaf.

4. Fold one side of the cabbage securely over the meat, then fold the thick end down over the meat. Continue rolling the cabbage until it is rolled tightly.

5. Tuck in the remaining cabbage end, poking it in securely with your finger.

6. Place the cabbage rolls in one layer, close together in a large casserole dish. Pour the meat juice mixture over the cabbage rolls.

7. Bake on 375 for 1 ½ hours or until the cabbage rolls are slightly browned on top. Serve hot.

Baba places the cabbage rolls close together in a large casserole dish. She pours the meat juice mixture over the cabbage rolls. They are ready to be put into the oven.

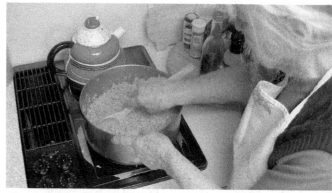

Baba dices the onion, places in large pot with the vegetable oil. She sautés until onion begins to brown. She adds ground meat and mixes, seasons with salt, pepper and Vegeta.

Baba explains to Damir to prepare a large pot, half full of water to boil. She cuts out the bottom core of the cabbage and discards outside leaves.

Baba drains excess juice from the meat and adds ingredients. Baba adds the egg and uncooked white rice to the meat stuffing and then stirs gently.

Baba teaches Damir to hold the cabbage leaf in the palm of one hand with the thick part of the leaf to the outside.

Damir puts 2 heaping tablespoons of meat in the center of the cabbage, forming a rectangle with a narrow end toward the outside, about 1" down the thick part of the leaf.

Baba folds one side of the cabbage securely over the meat, then folds the thick end down over the meat. She rolls the cabbage until it is rolled tightly.

Baba bakes on 375 for 1 ½ hours or until it is done. The tops of the cabbage rolls will be slightly brown.

There are hundreds of ways to make a schnitzel (I am exaggerating a bit) but my favorite is Karadjordje schnitzel. Chef Baba made it often in Yugoslavia but for whatever the reason, has seldom made it since we came to America. Making the schnitzel is actually easier than it looks—even I can do it from memory. But the taste is unbelievable; sophisticated enough for a king or queen.

Chef Baba made me realize that culture, food and history are intertwined. And knowing the history of a dish can make it even more enjoyable to eat. In the case of Karadjordje Schnitzel, I used to devour it as a child and teenager without even thinking about how it got its name. Karadjordje schnitzel was named after the Serbian prince Karađorđe. It is made with either rolled veal or pork steak with kajmak (which is a Serbian version of sour cream) and then breaded and fried. It is served with roasted potatoes and tartar sauce. The steak is sometimes referred to as "the maidens' dream" (devojački san), and I'll leave it to you to figure out why.

Although many of Chef Baba's recipes are hundreds of years old, this dish is a modern invention, created by chef Mića Stojanović in 1959, who, when he needed to prepare Chicken Kiev for a distinguished visitor from the Soviet Union, was faced with a lack of poultry. He used veal instead of chicken. However, not fully satisfied with the result, he poured tartar sauce over it, and decorated it with a slice of lemon and pieces of tomato, which at the end resembled the medal of the Order of the Star of Karađorđe, and thus the steak was named. Enjoy. It is amazingly delicious.

—Love, Damir
"Chef Baba's Sous Chef"

Karadjordje Schnitzel

Karadjordje's Schnitzel or Karadjordjeva šnicla, is a special breaded cutlet dish named after the Serbian Prince Karađorđe.

- Season 5
- Preparation Time: 40 minutes
- Baking time: 20 to 30 minutes
- Serves: 4

Ingredients:

    4 boneless pork loin cutlets
    2 teaspoons Vegeta
    4 tablespoons sour cream
    ½ carton (4 ounces) Egg Beaters
    2 cups all-purpose flour
    2 cups bread crumbs
    1 bottle of vegetable oil (Baba
        prefers safflower or sunflower oil)

Baba prepares to make a full meal, including the awesome Karadjordje Schnitzel.

Instructions:

1. Pound the cutlets with a meat hammer, until 1/4" thick. Sprinkle with Vegeta and allow to set for 15 minutes.

2. Dab 1 tablespoon of sour cream in the center of each cutlet. Roll the cutlets and set aside. Secure with wooden toothpicks if necessary.

3. Place the Egg Beaters, flour and bread crumbs in separate shallow bowls. Dip each rolled cutlets, to coat all sides, into the flour, then the Egg Beaters, then the bread crumbs.

4. Heat a 3" deep frying pan, filled with 2" of vegetable oil, over medium-high. When the oil is hot, add the schnitzels, seam-side down. Immediately reduce heat to medium and fry, turning the schnitzels frequently. They are done when they are nicely browned on all sides, in about 20 to 30 minutes.

5. Place the schnitzels on a plate lined with paper towels until ready to serve. Serve hot.

Baba prepares the ingredients.

Damir pounds the cutlets with a meat hammer, until ¼" thick. Sprinkle with Vegeta and allow to set for 15 minutes.

Baba places 1 tablespoon of sour cream in the center of each cutlet. Rolls the cutlets and sets them aside. Secures with the wooden toothpick, if necessary.

Baba places the Egg Beaters, flour and bread crumbs in separate shallow bowls. She dips each rolled cutlet, coats all sides, into the flour, then the Egg Beaters, then the bread crumbs.

Baba heats a 3" deep frying pan, filled with 2" of vegetable oil. When the oil is hot, she adds the schnitzels, seam-side down. Baba immediately reduces heat to medium and cooks them, turning the schnitzels frequently.

Baba prepares brussel sprouts as a side dish. (See recipe in the sides section of the cookbook.)

Baba prepares beets with garlic as a side dish.
(See recipe in the sides section of the cookbook.)

Baba prepares baked cauliflower as a side dish.
(See recipe in the sides section of the cookbook.)

Traditionally, you serve it with roasted potatoes and tartar sauce. Baba chose to change it up with baked sprouts, roasted cauliflower and beets.

"Baba, you cheated us in America. You should have made this every week while we were growing up," said Damir.

Karadjordje Schnitzel   105

Madeleine's first exposure to the Yugoslavian and Eastern European food culture. Her parents, Daniel Homeyer and Kristen Homeyer love it too.

Ćevapčići

These little skinless sausages are grilled and served with chopped onions. You can also add sour cream or Ajvar. One serving is typically 10 sausages served on flat bread or pita bread. It is so tasty even babies love Ćevapčiće. The Serbian or Croatian version is half pork and half beef. In Bosnia, this dish is typically made with beef and lamb.

- Season 4: Episode 8
- Preparation Time: 15 to 20 minutes
- Cooking Time: 16 to 18 minutes
- Serves 8-10
- Makes about 60 sausages

Ingredients:

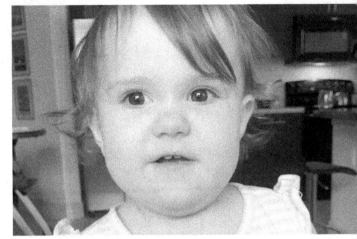

Madeleine Homeyer, the newest fan of Ćevapčići.

1 ½ pound ground sirloin beef
1 ½ pound ground pork, or lamb
4 cloves garlic, finely chopped
1 tablespoon salt (Chef Baba
  prefers Pink Himalayan salt)
1 teaspoon crushed red pepper
1 teaspoon paprika
1 tablespoon black pepper

CHEF BABA TIP: Wet your mixing hand just before mixing the meat so it does not stick to your hand.

Instructions:

1. Combine the beef and pork in a large mixing bowl. Add the garlic, salt, crushed red pepper, paprika and black pepper. Mix the meat and spices together with your hands. Mix the meat with one hand, while holding the bowl steady with the other hand. Mix by turning the meat over, then pressing down in the center of the meat with your fist. Continue until the spices and meat are thoroughly blended.

2. Make the sausages right away, or cover and refrigerate overnight. To make the sausages, take about 2 tablespoons of meat and roll between your hands to form a tube about 4 inches long and an inch thick. Make all of the sausages a uniform size. Line them up on a large cookie sheet to keep them separate.

3. Grill over medium heat for 16 to 18 minutes, turning frequently. Serve with finely chopped onion on pita bread.

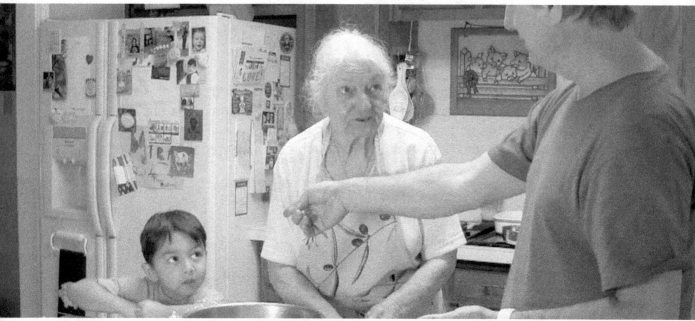

Baba combines the beef and pork in a bowl, then adds the garlic, salt, crushed red pepper, paprika and black pepper. She mixes the meat and spices together. Then she mixes by turning the meat over, pressing down in the center of the meat with her fist. Continues until the spices and meat are thoroughly blended.

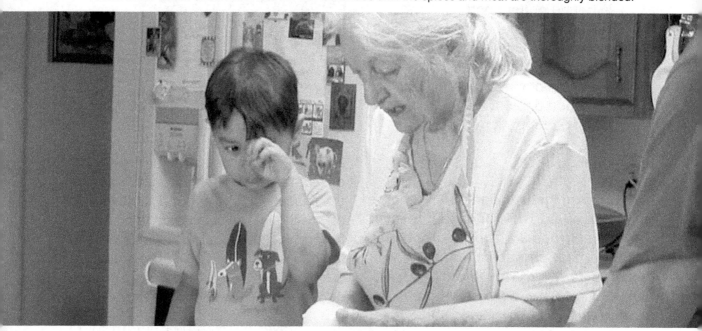

To make the sausages, Baba takes about 2 tablespoons of meat and rolls between her hands to form a tube about 4 inches long and an inch thick. She makes all of the sausages a uniform size. She lines them up on a large cookie sheet to keep them separate while Ivan sheds tears from the onion.

Damir grills the Ćevapčići over medium heat for 16 to 18 minutes, turning frequently.

Stuffed Peppers

Baba's version of the traditional Serbian recipe for Punjene Paprike. The combination of savory ground meat sautéed with onions with red, yellow or orange bell peppers is out of this world.

- Season 3: Episode 1
- Total Time to Make: 3 hours
- Serves: 8

Ingredients:

¼ large yellow onion
1 tablespoon vegetable oil (Baba uses safflower oil)
2 pounds ground beef, chicken or pork
1 teaspoon salt
½ teaspoon pepper
Vegeta
1 teaspoon paprika
8 large red or yellow bell peppers
1 egg
1 handful of white rice (uncooked)
8 round, raw potato slices, about ¼ to ½" thick
8 ounces tomato juice
1 cup tomato sauce

Instructions:

1. Dice the onion. Put into a large pot with the vegetable oil. Sauté over medium heat until the onion begins to brown. Add the ground meat and mix. Continue cooking over high heat, turning the meat as necessary to cook evenly. Adjust the temperature as needed. Season with salt, pepper and Vegeta to taste. The meat will be done in about 35 minutes.

2. Mix the paprika into the cooked meat. Taste to see if you want to adjust the seasoning. Set aside while you prepare the bell peppers.

3. Using a sharp knife, cut a 1" or 2" round hole in the top of each bell pepper to remove the stem, core and seeds. Set aside.

4. Add the egg and uncooked rice to the meat stuffing. Stir until mixed evenly. Fill each pepper with the meat stuffing. Place a slice of potato into the top hole of each pepper to keep the meat inside during baking.

5. Place the peppers, on their sides in a baking dish. Mix the tomato sauce with the tomato juice, and pour over the peppers. Cover with foil.

6. Bake at 375 degrees for about 2 hours or until peppers are tender. Serve hot or enjoy cold.

Baba dices the onion. Puts it into a large pot with the vegetable oil. Sautés over medium heat until the onion begins to brown. Adds the ground meat and mixes.

Baba adjusts the temperature as needed. Season with salt, pepper and Vegeta to taste. The meat will be done in about 35 minutes.

When the meat is done, Baba adds the paprika and mixes. Tastes to see if she wants to adjust the seasoning. Sets aside while she prepares the bell peppers.

Using a sharp knife, Damir cuts a 1" or 2" hole in the top of each bell pepper to remove the stem, core and seeds. Sets them aside.

Baba adds the egg and uncooked rice to the meat stuffing. Stirs until mixed evenly.

She fills each pepper with the meat stuffing.

Baba places a slice of potato into the top of each pepper to keep the meat inside during baking.

Chef Baba Tip: Never waste anything.

Baba shows how the potato covers the top hole of each pepper.

Baba places the peppers, on their sides in a baking dish.

She mixes the tomato sauce with the tomato juice, and pours over the peppers. Covers with foil.

Bakes at 375 for about 2 hours or until the peppers are tender. Serves hot or cold.

Ivo Perge, Chef Baba and Mira Paige Perge enjoying a lamb chop dinner.

Lamb Chops

Chef Baba's lamb chops are a great centerpiece to a traditional Serbian dinner with oven-fried potato wedges and salad.

- Season 4: Episode 6
- Preparation Time: 45 minutes
- Cooking Time: 30 to 40 minutes
- Serves: 10

Ingredients:

4 tablespoons olive oil
10 lamb chops
Dash of Vegeta (or salt)
Dash of pepper
10 medium garlic cloves
    (or 5 large cloves cut in half)

Instructions:

1. Preheat the oven to 375.

2. Add 2 tablespoons of olive oil to the bottom of a metal pan large enough that all of the chops will fit in one layer.

3. Wash the lamb chops, and pat dry. Season with vegeta and pepper. With a small, sharp knife, make a cut in the center of each chop, and tuck a whole garlic clove inside of each one.

4. Place the lamb chops in one layer in the pan. Brush with olive oil. Allow to marinate for 20 to 30 minutes.

5. Bake at 375 degrees for about 45 minutes.

Oven Fried Potato Wedges

- Preparation Time: 15 minutes
- Cooking Time: 45 minutes
- Serves: 4 to 6

Ingredients:

4 or 5 large russet potatoes
1 ½ to 2 cups sunflower oil
2 tablespoons Vegeta

Instructions:

1. Cut each potato into 6 length-wise wedges, ½" to 1" thick. Pat the potatoes dry with a paper towel. Toss with 2 tablespoons of sunflower oil and Vegeta seasoning.

2. Pour sunflower oil into a baking pan to about ½" deep. Place the pan in the oven and preheat to 375 degrees. When oven is preheated, remove pan of oil and add the potatoes to the pan.

3. Bake the potatoes for about 20 minutes, or until they are tender. Remove from the oven, toss with a spatula. Continue baking until the edges are brown and crispy. When Baba serves these potatoes they disappear very fast.

Baba adds 2 tablespoons of olive oil to the bottom of a metal pan large enough that all of the chops will fit in one layer.

She washes the lamb chops, and pats dry. Seasons with Vegeta and pepper, makes a cut in the center of each chop, and tucks a whole garlic clove inside.

Damir places the lamb chops in one layer in the pan. Brushes with olive oil. Allows to marinate for 20 to 30 minutes.

Baba grills or bakes at 375 for about 45 minutes.

Damir cuts each potato into 6 length-wise wedges, ½" to 1" thick. Pats the potatoes dry with a paper towel. Tosses with 2 tablespoons of sunflower oil and Vegeta.

Damir pours oil into a baking pan to about ½" deep. Places the pan in the oven and preheats to 375 degrees. When the oven is preheated, removes the pan of oil and adds the potatoes to the pan.

Chef Baba

Baba bakes the potatoes for about 20 minutes, or until they are tender. Removes from the oven, tosses with a spatula. Continues baking until the edges are brown and crispy.

Baba and Damir prepare Baba's Magic Salad, which helped her lose sixty pounds in less then twelve months

Damir discusses what kind of Baba's healthy eating plan he can do in order to get back to his optimal soccer weight.

Perfect match: Baba's Oven-Fried Potato Wedges, Baba's Magic Salad and lamb chops.

Baba teaches Damir to tenderize the pork correctly.

Damir recalls how much he loved eating pork schnitzel when Baba made it for Sunday lunch in Yugoslavia.

Every year after the corn harvest in Yugoslavia, just before the first frost hit the grass on our beautiful ranch in Sremska Mitrovica, my husband Ivan would kill one of our pigs to make his famous pork sausage. This was our yearly family tradition. And this is a yearly tradition of many families in the Eastern European culture.

Ivan could make a mean sausage. He did not like to cook but he was an expert at making sausage. And he made good Šljivovica, a famous Yugoslavian plum brandy. Making sausage and consuming Šljivovica for an entire day was "something you do" in our culture.

Ivan had a gift for cutting meat. Nothing was ever wasted from our pig. Every piece of the pig was carved up, to be eaten over the course of the following year. He especially loved eating the tongue. Pig's feet were considered a delicacy, and we both loved eating them.

We also enjoyed making pork schnitzel after a long day of making sausage. And it would not be a complete meal if this delicious pork schnitzel were not accompanied with my mashed potatoes and creamed spinach. It tastes "more than good." It is "Babalicious."

—Love, Chef Baba

Pork Schnitzel

Make a traditional Eastern European dinner with these tender schnitzels, Baba's Mashed Potatoes and Creamed Spinach.

- Season 3: Episode 3
- Total Time to Make: 35 to 40 minutes
- Serves: 4

Ingredients:

4 pork loin cutlets
Vegeta seasoning
Vegetable oil (Baba uses
  sunflower oil)
2 cups all-purpose flour
2 cups Egg Beaters
2 cups bread crumbs

Instructions:

1. Tenderize each cutlet by pounding with a meat hammer, on both sides, until about ¼" thick. Season both sides of each cutlet with Vegeta.

2. Heat the vegetable oil, ½" deep, over medium high in a large skillet. Put the flour, Egg Beaters and bread crumbs into 3 separate bowls. One at a time, place the cutlets in the flour to coat both sides, dip into the Egg Beaters to coat evenly, then place in the bread crumbs and shake gently to coat one side then the other.

3. Test the oil for frying. The oil is ready if, when you add a drop of Egg Beaters,

Baba's Mashed Potatoes, Baba's Creamed Spinach and Pork Schnitzel.

it forms a ball and sizzles. One or two at a time, carefully place each pork loin in the oil and fry for 4 minutes on each side until browned. Lift the pork loin out using a fork, allowing any excess oil to fall off. Place on a plate lined with a paper towel. Serve hot.

Baba's Mashed Potatoes

Ingredients:

4 large white potatoes (Baba's
favorite are Mountain
King potatoes)*
1 pinch of salt
⅓ cup milk
½ stick butter
1 teaspoon Vegeta
1 teaspoon salt

Instructions:

1. Wash the potatoes and place them in a large pot. Cover completely with cold water. Add a pinch of salt. Cover and bring to a boil. Reduce the heat to low and boil for 20 minutes. The potatoes are done when they are tender when poked with a fork.

2. Remove the potatoes from heat and drain off the water. Allow them to cool slightly, then peel off the potato skin and place the potatoes back in the pot.

CHEF BABA TIP: The potatoes are easier to peel while hot. Avoid burning your fingers. Use a folded paper towel to grasp the hot potato in one hand and carefully peel off the skin with the other.

3. Pour the milk into a small bowl. Cut the butter into slices and add to the milk. Heat for 1 minute on high in the microwave.

4. Mash the potatoes, adding the Vegeta and milk-butter mixture gradually. Taste to see if you need more seasoning.

Baba's Creamed Spinach

Ingredients:

1 pound fresh spinach
½ cup cooking oil (Baba uses
sunflower or corn oil)
2 tablespoons all-purpose flour
2 or 3 cloves garlic, chopped
½ cups whole milk
1 tablespoon Vegeta

Instructions:

1. Fill a large pot about 2/3 full of water and bring to a boil. Add the spinach and stir gently with large spoon. As soon as the spinach becomes limp, remove from the heat and set aside.

2. Combine the oil, flour and garlic in a medium sauce pan. Stir over medium heat until hot, reduce to low heat and continue stirring until browned.

3. Drain the spinach and place on a chopping board. Chop the spinach, add to the pan with the oil-flour mixture and mix over medium heat. Add the milk and stir. Add the vegeta. Stir the spinach gently over low heat until the milk is absorbed.

4. Remove from heat and place into a serving bowl. Serve hot.

*Visit http://mountainking.com

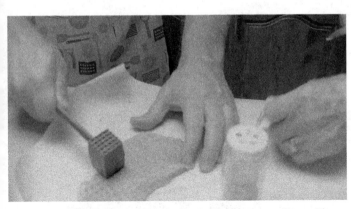

Damir tenderizes each cutlet by pounding with a meat hammer, on both sides, until about ¼" thick. Seasons both sides of each cutlet with Vegeta.

Baba puts the flour, Egg Beaters and bread crumbs into 3 separate bowls.

In a large skillet, Baba heats vegetable oil, ½" deep, over medium high.

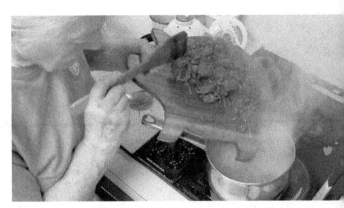

Baba fills a large pot about 2/3 full of water and brings it to a boil. She adds the chopped spinach and stirs gently with large spoon.

Adds the milk and stirs. Adds the Vegeta. Stirs the spinach gently over low heat until the milk is absorbed.

Baba cuts the butter into slices and adds it to the milk, heats it for 1 minute on high in the microwave. Mashes the potatoes, adding the Vegeta and milk-butter mixture gradually.

Baba's Chicken Chili

This hearty recipe was chosen as the best chili recipe of all at one of Chef Baba's large family gatherings. Chef Baba was inspired to create a fusion of ingredients from Texas and Yugoslavian cultures.

- Season 4: Episode 4
- Total Time to Make: 1 hour
- Serves: 4 to 6

Ingredients:

½ large white onion
½ large green bell pepper
1 large clove of garlic
2 tablespoons olive oil
2 pinches of salt (Baba recommends pink Himalayan salt)
1/2 fresh jalapeño
1 pound ground chicken
1 teaspoon chili powder
1 teaspoon crushed red pepper
2 (10-ounce) cans diced tomatoes with green chilies
1 (15-ounce) can kidney beans (or pinto beans), undrained
1 (8-ounce) can tomato sauce
Mozzarella cheese and green onions for garnish

Family party in Austin, Texas: Goldie Radojević, Dejan Perge and Nina Radojević Kelly

Instructions:

1. Dice the onion and green bell pepper. Add the olive oil into a large, deep pot. Add the garlic, olive oil and a pinch of salt. Heat over medium heat until the peppers are tender and onion is translucent.

2. Add the ground chicken and stir. Add a pinch of salt. Stir in the chili powder and crushed red pepper. Stir the chicken occasionally to cook evenly.

3. Chop the jalapeño (remove the seeds if you want less spicy chili) and add to the pot.

4. When the chicken is cooked, stir in the diced tomatoes with green chilies, beans (do not drain), and tomato sauce.

CHEF BABA TIP: For even thicker chili, use just one can of diced tomatoes.

5. Simmer on low heat for 20 minutes.

6. Garnish with shredded mozzarella cheese and green onions and serve hot.

While Damir is cutting the onion, Jon Perge is backseat driving him on how to do it.

Baba joins Jon in carefully monitoring his cutting of the onion.

Jon takes over and dices the onion and green bell pepper. Adds the olive oil into a large, deep pot. Adds the garlic, olive oil and a pinch of salt.

Baba heats the chili over medium heat until the peppers are tender and onion is translucent.

Baba adds the ground chicken and stirs. Adds a pinch of salt. Stirs in the chili powder and crushed red pepper. Stirs the chicken occasionally to cook evenly.

When the chicken is cooked, Baba stirs in the diced tomatoes with green chilies, beans (do not drain), and tomato sauce. Simmers on low heat for 20 minutes.

Baba's Chicken Chili is a fusion between Slavic
and Texas cooking traditions.

Beef Wellington

This is one of Chef Baba's all-time favorite entrees. Here is her version of this international favorite dish.

- Season 5
- Preparation Time: 1 hour
- Cooking Time: 55 minutes
- Serves 8 to 10

Ingredients:

Frozen puff pastry sheet
   (Pepperidge Farm or from your
   local European grocery store)
3 pound trimmed fillet of beef
Salt and pepper to taste
Vegetable oil (olive, sunflower or
   safflower oil)
¼ cup chopped fresh mushrooms
1 tablespoon butter
1 tablespoon Šljivovica (plum
   brandy)
1 cup prepared or canned liver pâté
1 egg, beaten

Instructions:

1. Thaw the puff pastry and set aside.

2. Preheat oven to 400 degrees.

3. Wash and trim any fat from the fillet. Season with salt and pepper and brush with oil. Place the fillet on the rack in a roasting pan. Roast for 30 minutes at 400 degrees, for rare. Remove from oven and allow to cool to room temperature.

4. Add the chopped mushrooms and butter to a skillet. Heat over high for 1 minute, stirring continuously. Add Šljivovica and continue cooking until most of the liquid has evaporated. Remove from heat, add to the pâté and mix well. Spread the mixture on top of the fillet.

5. Using a rolling pin, roll the pastry into a rectangle less than ¼" thick. Place the fillet, with the pâté mixture on the bottom, lengthwise on the pastry. Wrap the pastry around the fillet, overlapping the edges to form a seam. Moisten the edges to seal. Trim the top layer of the pastry from the ends, and fold up over the fillet. Moisten the edges to seal.

6. Lightly spray a cooking sheet with cooking oil. Carefully place the wrapped fillet onto the cooking sheet, seam side down. Brush the pastry with the beaten egg. Refrigerate.

7. Bring to room temperature before serving. Brush again with egg. Bake at 425 for 25 minutes, or until the pastry is golden. Remove from oven and let stand for 10 minutes before carving.

Baba trims any fat from the fillet. Seasons with salt and pepper and brushes with oil. Places the fillet in a roasting pan. Roasts for 30 minutes at 400 degrees, for rare.

Jon Dylan Perge chops the mushrooms and adds them with butter to a skillet. Heats over high for 1 minute. Adds brandy and continues cooking until most of the liquid has evaporated.

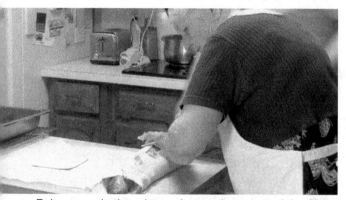

Baba spreads the mixture Jon made on top of the fillet. Using a rolling pin, rolls the pastry into a rectangle less than ¼" thick. Places the fillet, with the pâté mixture on the bottom, lengthwise on the pastry.

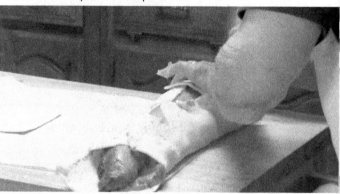

She wraps the pastry around the fillet, overlapping the edges to form a seam. Moistens the edges to seal. Trims the top layer of the pastry from the ends, and folds up over the fillet.

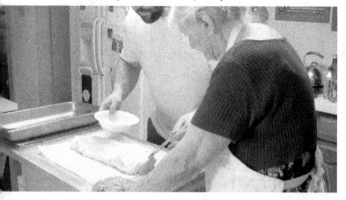

She lightly sprays a cooking sheet with cooking oil. Carefully places the wrapped fillet onto the cooking sheet, seam side down. Jon brushes the pastry with the beaten egg. Refrigerates it.

Before serving, Baba brings it to room temperature. Brushes again with egg. Bakes at 425 for 25 minutes, or until the pastry is golden. Removes from oven and lets it stand for 10 minutes before Jon begins carving.

Jon Dylan and Chef Baba celebrating her 85th birthday.

Chef Baba's family and friends Harkins Chan and Vinh Nguyen celebrate her 85th birthday.

Beef Wellington   129

Grilled Pork Chops with Onions

A simple Slavic recipe that is amazingly delicious. The freshly grilled pork is shaken in diced onions so they go together perfectly. Baba recommends serving this with either cabbage salad, tomato salad or green salad.

- Season 5
- Preparation Time: 15 minutes
- Cooking Time: 15 to 20
- Serves: 4

Ingredients:

1 pork tenderloin (or 8 pork chops)
1 tablespoon Vegeta (or salt)
2 white onions, finely chopped
2 teaspoons black pepper
2 tablespoons cooking oil
  (safflower or sunflower)
Cooking oil spray

Wash the tenderloin and pat dry with a paper towel. Sprinkle with Vegeta. Cover loosely with a paper towel and allow the pork to rest, absorbing the spices for 15 to 30 minutes.

Instructions:

1. Wash the pork and dry with a paper towel. Sprinkle both sides with Vegeta, and rub into the meat. Cover and set aside for 30 minutes to one hour.

2. Slice the pork loin into 1" thick cuts. Place in a bowl, toss the pork with black pepper and cooking oil.

3. Spray your grill with cooking oil. Heat your outdoor gas grill on medium-high heat. Sear the pork 2 to 3 minutes on each side. Lower the heat to medium. Cook until pork is done, about 15 minutes, turning half way through cooking.

Sear the chops for 2 to 3 minutes on each side, then lower the heat to medium. Continue cooking until chops are done, about 15 minutes, turning half way through cooking.

4. Place the onions in a large covered dish. Add the hot pork, cover and shake until onions are a light brown.

5. Serve the pork on a bed of the onion.

Baba's Baked Trout

Simplicity is the key to Chef Baba's cooking and this is a simple and delicious way to bake trout or other white fish.

- Season 5
- Preparation Time: 10 minutes
- Cooking Time: 15 minutes
- Serves: 8

Ingredients:

8 fresh trout fillets (or other white fish)
1 to 2 teaspoons salt
1 to 2 teaspoons pepper
Juice of 1 lemon (optional)

Instructions:

1. Preheat the oven to 375 degrees.

2. Wash the fish and pat dry with a paper towel.

3. Add the salt, pepper and optional lemon to both sides of the fish. Line a baking sheet with foil.

4. Arrange the fish in one layer on the baking sheet.

5. Bake at 375 for 15 minutes, depending on oven.

Damir thinks it is one of the simplest dishes I make, but he says "It is still so damn delicious." He added my Ajvar and mashed sweet potatoes to his plate.

Baba washes the fish and pat dries it with a paper towel. She adds the salt, pepper and optional lemon to both sides of the fish. Line a baking sheet with foil.

Baba bakes the fish at 375 for 15 minutes, but baking time depends on your oven.

As a boy in Yugoslavia, there was one thing I loved almost as much as playing soccer in the neighborhood, or running the highly dangerous beams of the unfinished mansion my grandfather was building before he left for America—it was fishing with my cousin Zdenko Perge.

Zdenko loved playing soccer with me and my twin brother, but after playing to exhaustion, we would go to the back of our farmhouse, to our large garden and dig up worms galore. I have never in my life seen a garden with so many worms. I was a little queasy about touching worms, but Zdenko helped me get over it quickly. They were just worms. Great for irrigation and great for catching fish.

As the sun began to set, we would walk the two hundred meters from our ranch to find our fishing spot in a large pond. Just to circle the pond took five minutes on my bike.

For someone only a few years older than I was, Zdenko was a smart fisherman. He taught me how to place the worms on the hook and swing the fishing rod correctly. And he taught me to catch a lot of fish by being extremely patient. Zdenko held the fishing pole lightly so when the fish nibbled, he could snap his wrist and catch the fish.

After the sun set, we would return to the farmhouse where Chef Baba would fry the fish so we could share the spoils with the entire family. It was delicious.

—Love, Damir
"Chef Baba's Sous Chef"

Chef Baba

Baba's Fried Catfish

This recipe is wonderful for catfish, trout or your favorite white fish. The fish will be light and flaky with a delicate crust.

- Season 5
- Preparation Time: 20 minutes
- Cooking Time: 15 minutes
- Serves: 8

Ingredients:

8 fresh fish fillets
   (catfish, trout, other white fish)
2 tablespoons cooking oil
1 to 2 teaspoons salt
1 to 2 teaspoons ground pepper
Juice of one fresh lemon
2 cups all-purpose flour
½ carton (8-ounces) Egg Beaters
1 bottle vegetable oil

Instructions:

1. Wash the fish and pat dry with a paper towel. Brush the fish with vegetable oil. Sprinkle both sides with salt, pepper and lemon juice.

2. Place the flour and Egg Beaters in two separate bowls large enough to dip the fish. Dip each piece of fish in the flour to coat, then the Egg Beaters, then again in the flour. Place the fish on a large platter.

CHEF BABA TIP: For a tasty alternative, dip the fish in ground pecans, in place of the second coating of flour.

Damir plates the food as Chef Baba's Sous Chef. He prefers this function much more than washing dishes.

3. Add vegetable oil, 2 ½" deep, into a deep skillet. Heat the oil to 365 degrees. Place a few fillets in the oil to fry, so not to be crowded. Fry until golden brown on both sides, about 3 minutes. The fish should be light and flaky on the inside. Remove from the frying pan and place on paper towel to absorb excess oil. Serve hot with horseradish sauce.

Baba's Roasted Turkey

Cooking simplicity at its best, and this turkey recipe is proof. Amazingly tender and juicy. As Baba says, "More than good."

- Season 5
- Preparation Time: 1 hour
- Baking time: 2 ½ to 3 hours
- Serves: 10 to 12

Ingredients:

1 fresh turkey (Baba prefers
    Honeysuckle White brand)
2 or 3 tablespoon Vegeta (or
    paprika or ground pepper)
1 stick of unsalted butter
¼ vegetable oil (sunflower or
    safflower oil)

Instructions:

1. Wash the turkey and pat dry with paper towels. Sprinkle with Vegeta all over, inside and out. Allow the turkey to set for one hour.

2. Rub the turkey with butter on the outside. Using your fingers, loosen the skin at the neck. Grab the skin with one hand and work in your other hand to loosen the skin down to the thighs and legs. Place pats of butter all under the skin.

3. Preheat the oven to 400 degrees.

4. Add the vegetable oil to the roasting pan, set the turkey in the pan breast-side

Baba prepares to roast the Turkey for Thanksgiving 2017.

up and place in oven. Baste every 15 minutes with the oil and juices at the bottom of the pan. The turkey will be a rich, golden brown. The interior temperature should reach 180 degrees when done.

5. Remove from oven and allow the turkey to rest for 20 minutes before carving.

Baba prepares to bake pork loin.

Angela, Baba and Jana in the kitchen.

Damir prepares to cut the turkey.

Damir loves using knives.

Damir cuts the main event: turkey.

Baba's Famous Chicken Noodle Soup.

Baba always prepares a green salad.

Ivan and Danijela Perge waiting to feast.

Roasted Bell Peppers. Yum.

Pork loin and baked potatoes.

Salad, stuffing & sweet mashed potatoes.

Jelena waiting for her soup.

Angela and Dejan Perge.

Jana Arnold at Thanksgiving.

Damir's job is to serve the soup.

For those that prefer tomato soup.

Russian Chicken Salad. Aaaaahhhhhh.

Turkey stuffing.

Turkey gizzard stuffing.

Sweet potatoes and stuffing.

Ivan loves Baba's soup.

Danijela and Luka looking for seconds.

Baba helps Ivan with his soup.

Roasted Bell Peppers.

Damir's Krempita frenemy: Luka Perge.

Angela Perge and Danny Perge discuss the feast.

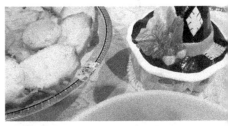

Thanksgiving decoration with pork loin.

God, I mean Chef Baba, made the mashed potatoes.

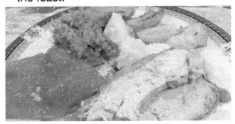

Damir's plate of heaven.

Baba asks Damir to cut the Krempita.

Krempita. Yes, it was completely devoured within minutes. Estimated time: 2:34 seconds.

Krempita's friends, waiting for their turn. These wonderful cookies had to wait until the Krempita was gone. It didn't take long for everyone to get to them.

Coconut Bars.

Voćna Salama.

OMG: Krempita.

Ivan is trying to figure out where to start because there is only so much space in his tummy.

Jana, Mira Paige, Jelena, Baba, Angela, Ivan, Danijela and Luka prepare for the holiday feast.

Chef Baba

Chicken Paprikaš

A traditional favorite that can be prepared with homemade dumplings (recipe below) or Baba's homemade noodles.

- Total Time to Make: about 1 hour
- Serves: 6 to 8

Ingredients:

> 1 large white onion, chopped
> ¼ cup vegetable oil (sunflower, safflower or olive oil)
> 1 (4-pound) chicken, cut up
> 1 tablespoon sweet red paprika
> 1 to 2 cups water
> 1 teaspoon Vegeta (or salt)

Instructions:

1. Wash the chicken and pat dry. Cover the bottom of a deep sauce pan with vegetable oil. Add the onion and sauté over low heat until translucent. Mix the red paprika into the onions. Add the chicken pieces and enough water to cover the chicken. Cover and cook on medium heat or until sauce thickens, about 30 minutes. As it cooks add water as needed to keep the chicken covered.

2. Add Vegeta and salt. Continue cooking for another 30 minutes, stirring occasionally. The chicken should be tender, and lightly brown on both sides. Prepare dumplings (recipe below) or noodles while chicken is cooking.

Noodles instructions: If you use store bought noodles, prepare them al dente.

CHEF BABA TIP: You can cook the chicken in a slow cooker on medium or low for 2 to 6 hours if you choose.

3. When chicken is done, pour the chicken and sauce over the dumplings or noodles in a serving dish. Enjoy!

Dumpling Recipe Ingredients:

> 2 eggs
> 1 tablespoon shortening
> 1 teaspoon salt
> ½ cup water
> 1 ¾ to 2 cups all-purpose flour

1. Stir together the eggs, shortening and salt in a medium mixing bowl. Add the water and mix. Add the flour gradually, ½ cup at a time, as you mix using a spatula. The dough should be smooth, and just thick enough to hold its shape when scooped with a spoon.

2. Fill a large saucepan ¾ full of water and bring to a boil. Add the dough, one heaping tablespoon spoonful at time to the boiling water. It should stay clumped together, if not, add a little more flour to the dough. The dumplings will swell, and all will rise to the top when they are done. Remove from water with a slotted spoon and place in a serving dish.

Chicken Paprikaš 143

Chef Baba

Side Dishes

It is difficult to categorize Chef Baba's Ajvar, Roasted Bell Peppers or Scalloped Potatoes as side dishes because they have been worshipped by her family as their true delights in their own right.

Baba's Ajvar

Ajvar or Serbian Roasted Red Pepper Spread. Ajvar is delicious by itself or added to a sausage sandwich.

- Season 5
- Preparation Time: 20 minutes
- Cooking Time: 30 minutes

Ingredients:

10 large red bell peppers
1 large eggplant
1 1/2 teaspoons salt
1 to 3 teaspoons crushed red
  pepper flakes (to taste)
1 teaspoon black pepper (to taste)
2 garlic cloves, freshly minced
2 teaspoons sunflower oil or
  safflower oil
1 tablespoon white vinegar

Instructions:

1. Preheat the oven to 375 degrees. Place the whole bell peppers on a sheet of foil, on the top rack of the oven. Bake until the peppers are blackened on all sides, turning as one side becomes blackened. About 30 minutes. Do not overbake.

2. Remove the peppers from the oven. Place them in a large bowl, covered, for 20 to 30 minutes to loosen the skin. Re-

move the skin. Pull out the core, seeds and all. Open the peppers and cut in half.

3. Pierce the skin of the eggplant and wrap in foil to preserve the color while baking.

4. Bake for about 30 minutes until the eggplant is soft all over. Remove from oven. Place in a wooden bowl. Using two wooden spoons, break apart the eggplant in small pieces.

CHEF BABA TIP: Use a wooden bowl and spoon with the eggplant to help preserve the color.

5. Add the roasted red peppers to the eggplant. Mix thoroughly. Strain off excess juice.

CHEF BABA TIP: The excess pepper juice is nice to mix with vodka.

6. Run the roasted red peppers and eggplant through a food processor.

7. Place the Ajvar in a wooden bowl. Add the salt, crushed red pepper and black pepper. Mix thoroughly. Add the garlic and sunflower oil. Taste and adjust the spices as necessary, adding more garlic or crushed red pepper if desired.

8. Allow to cool overnight at room temperature, or for at least 2 hours in the refrigerator. Place in a jar until ready to serve.

146 Baba's Ajvar

Baba's Roasted Peppers

Paprika or Roasted Red Peppers with Garlic. They can be eaten as a delicious salad, or add a slice of the roasted red pepper to your next sandwich. This simple recipe is a true Balkan staple.

- Season 5
- Preparation Time: 30 minutes
- Cooking Time: 30 minutes

Ingredients:

> 5 bell peppers (red, yellow
>   or orange)
> 6 or 7 garlic cloves, chopped
> ½ cup olive oil
> 2 to 3 teaspoons salt (to taste)

Roasted Peppers with garlic.

Instructions:

1. Preheat the oven to 375 degrees. Place the whole bell peppers on a sheet of foil, on the top rack of the oven. Bake until the peppers are blackened on all sides, turning as one side becomes blackened. About 30 minutes. Do not over bake.

2. Remove the peppers from the oven. Place them in a large bowl, covered, for 20 to 30 minutes to loosen the skin. Remove the skin. Pull out the core, seeds and all. Open the peppers and cut in half.

3. Place the roasted peppers in 4 layers, adding a little salt, garlic and olive oil between each layer.

4. Refrigerate the roasted peppers overnight. Serve or store in airtight jars for later.

Chef Baba used roasted bell peppers and potato salad to enhance the delicious fried catfish.

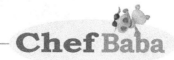
Baba's Creamed Spinach

A rich creamy dish that fits well with mashed potatoes and pork schnitzel to create a traditional Eastern European dinner.

- Season 3: Episode 3
- Total Time to Make: 30 minutes
- Serves 4

Ingredients:

1 pound fresh spinach
½ cup cooking oil (Baba uses sunflower or corn oil)
2 tablespoons all-purpose flour
2 or 3 cloves garlic, chopped
½ cups whole milk
1 tablespoon Vegeta

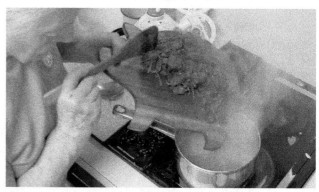

Fill a large pot about ⅔ full of water and bring to a boil. Add the spinach and stir gently with a large spoon.

Instructions:

1. Fill a large pot about 2/3 full of water and bring to a boil. Add the spinach and stir gently with large spoon. As soon as the spinach becomes limp, remove from the heat and set aside.

2. Combine the oil, flour and garlic in a medium sauce pan. Stir over medium heat until hot, reduce to low heat and continue stirring until browned.

3. Drain the spinach and place on a chopping board. Chop the spinach, add to the pan with the oil-flour mixture and mix over medium heat. Add the milk and stir. Add the vegeta. Stir the spinach

As soon as the spinach becomes limp, remove from the heat and set aside.

gently over low heat until the milk is absorbed.

4. Remove from heat and place into a serving bowl. Serve hot.

Baba's Mashed Potatoes

Baba's mashed potatoes are so perfect that they don't need gravy. Enjoy them with Pork Schnitzel, Beef Wellington, or any of Chef Baba's meat dishes.

- Season 3: Episode 3
- Preparation time: 15 minutes
- Cooking Time: 20 to 30 minutes
- Serves: 4

Ingredients:

> 4 large white potatoes (Baba's favorite are Mountain King potatoes)*
> 1 pinch of salt
> 1/3 cup milk
> ½ stick butter
> 1 teaspoon Vegeta
> 1 teaspoon salt

Baba mashes the potatoes, adding the Vegeta and milk-butter mixture gradually.

Instructions:

1. Wash the potatoes and place them in a large pot. Cover completely with cold water. Add a pinch of salt. Cover and bring to a boil. Reduce the heat to low and boil for 20 minutes. The potatoes are done when they are tender when poked with a fork.

2. Remove the potatoes from heat and drain off the water. Allow them to cool slightly, then peel off the potato skin and place the potatoes back in the pot.

*Visit http://mountainking.com

CHEF BABA TIP: The potatoes are easier to peel while hot. Avoid burning your fingers. Use a folded paper towel to grasp the hot potato in one hand and carefully peel off the skin with the other.

3. Pour the milk into a small bowl. Cut the butter into slices and add to the milk. Heat for 1 minute on high in the microwave.

4. Mash the potatoes, adding the Vegeta and milk-butter mixture gradually. Taste to see if you need more seasoning. Serve hot.

Baba's Peas

These tender peas, flavored with parsley and Vegeta, are a delicious complement to any traditional Eastern European meal.

- Season 3: Episode 5
- Preparation time: 5 minutes
- Cooking Time: 25
- Serves: 4

Ingredients:

> 2 (10-ounce) bags frozen peas
>   (thawed) or fresh peas
> ¼ cup chopped Italian parsley
> 1 tablespoon olive oil
> 1 cup water
> 1 heaping tablespoon
>   all-purpose flour
> ½ to 1 teaspoon Vegeta

Instructions:

1. Place the peas in a skillet or shallow pan, add the parsley and olive oil. Add ½ cup water and stir. Cover and cook at medium heat, stirring occasionally, until the peas are tender, about 10 or 15 minutes.

2. Sprinkle flour over the peas, add ½ cup water. Stir gently over medium heat until the sauce is thick and creamy. Reduce the heat to low. Mix in the Vegeta and cook for 1 additional minute. Remove the peas from the heat. Cover until ready to serve.

Baba places the peas in a skillet or shallow pan, adds the parsley and olive oil. Adds ½ cup water and stirs.

After the peas are tender, Baba sprinkles flour over the peas, adds ½ cup water. Stirs gently over medium heat until the sauce is thick and creamy. Reduces the heat to low. Mixes in the vegeta and cooks for 1 additional minute. She remove the peas from the heat.

Baba's Red Cabbage

Braised red cabbage. Simply delicious.

- Season 3: Episode 5
- Preparation Time: 10 minutes
- Cooking Time: 25 minutes
- Serves: 4

Ingredients:

½ large red cabbage
1 to 2 tablespoons olive oil
½ cup water
1 teaspoon white vinegar

Instructions:

1. Cut the cabbage in half. Cut out and discard the core. Slice the cabbage into ½" pieces.

2. Heat the olive oil in a large, heavy pot over medium heat until simmering. Add the cabbage, cover and cook, stirring occasionally until it is tender and bright purple.

3. Add the water and vinegar, mix. Continue simmering until the liquid is absorbed. Serve hot.

Heat the olive oil in a large, heavy pot over medium heat until simmering. Add the cabbage, cover and cook, stirring occasionally until it is tender and bright purple.

Baba cuts the cabbage in half. Cuts out and discards the core. Slices the cabbage into ½" pieces.

Damir learns how to cut the cabbage like a professional chef—like Chef Baba.

Bećarac

Bećarac is a tasty tomato dish that can be served hot or cold, and it's good for you.

- Season 5
- Preparation Time: 15 minutes
- Cooking Time: 35 to 40 minutes
- Serves: 6 to 8

Ingredients:

> 1 white onion, diced
> 2 tablespoons olive oil
> 1 large bell pepper (red, yellow or
>   orange), cut into 1" wide strips
> 2 large or 4 medium tomatoes
> 1 tablespoon Vegeta

Instructions:

1. Add the onion and vegetable oil to a large sauce pan and sauté over medium high, covered, for about 10 minutes. When the onions are translucent, add the bell pepper. Reduce heat to medium, cover and continue cooking until the peppers are tender, about 10 more minutes.

2. Run hot water over the tomatoes for 2 minutes to loosen the skin. Peel off the skin, and slice the tomatoes. Add to the onions and peppers, stir and continue cooking. If the tomatoes are too watery, add 1 tablespoon of flour to thicken. Add the Vegeta and mix. Cover and continue cooking, stirring occasionally for another

Bećarac is tasty tomato dish that can be served hot or cold, and goes with everything.

20 to 30 minutes, or until the tomatoes are cooked and the Bećarac becomes like a sauce.

3. Enjoy hot or cold.

Baba's Scalloped Potatoes

A simple and delicious potato recipe. You can add bacon, sausage or pork ribs to the top of the potatoes before baking to make a complete meal when accompanied by a salad.

- Season 5
- Preparation Time: 20 minutes
- Baking time: 45 minutes to 1 hour
- Serves: 4 to 6

Ingredients:

4 large potatoes
1 large white onion, diced
1 tablespoon sweet red paprika
1 tablespoon Vegeta (or salt)
1 ½ to 2 cups water

Baba bakes the potatoes for 45 minutes.

The potatoes should brown on the edges.

Instructions:

1. Wash the potatoes and remove the skin. Slice into ¼" thick slices. Add the Vegeta and mix. Set aside.

2. Sauté the onion until translucent. Remove from heat and add 1 tablespoon paprika and stir.

3. Preheat oven to 375 degrees.

4. In a casserole dish, add the onions in an even layer on the bottom. Add the potatoes evenly over the onions. Add enough water to just cover the potatoes.

5. Bake at 375 for 45 minutes to one hour, or until the potatoes are tender and beginning to brown on the edges and the water is absorbed. Enjoy hot!

Chef Baba made scalloped potatoes with cabbage salad, grilled asparagus and baked flounder for Paige, Ivan, Jana and Damir in less then 50 minutes. And let's not forget she also made white bean soup.

Baba's Beets with Garlic

This true Balkan favorite is a good accompaniment to pork.

- Season 5
- Preparation Time:
- Serves: 4 to 6

Ingredients:

5 or 6 fresh beets
2 dashes of salt
4 cloves garlic, freshly chopped
¼ cup extra virgin olive oil
2 tablespoons vinegar (white or
    red wine vinegar)

Instructions:

1. Boil the beets, covered, until just tender when poked with a fork, about 30 to 45 minutes. Drain off water and allow to cool slightly so you can peel off the skin. Cut the beets into ¼" thick slices.

2. Layer half of the beets in the bottom of a casserole dish. Sprinkle with one dash of salt and 2 chopped garlic cloves. Layer the remaining beets, spread evenly. Sprinkle with a dash of salt and remaining garlic.

3. Cover the beets with the vegetable oil and vinegar. Allow the beets to marinate for 24 hours inside the refrigerator, or at room temp. Serve.

Baba boils the beets for about 30-45 minutes.

Damir cuts the beets into ¼" thick slices.

Ivan shows up to supervise Damir's cutting.

Sprinkles with salt and 2 chopped garlic cloves.

Baba covers the beets with vegetable oil and vinegar.

Beets complement Karadjordjeva Schnitzel.

Baba's Baked Cauliflower

You've never had cauliflower so crispy and light. It will melt in your mouth.

- Season 5
- Preparation Time: 15 minutes
- Baking time: 30 minutes
- Serves: 4 to 6

Ingredients:

1 large cauliflower head
3 to 4 tablespoons olive oil
1 tablespoon Vegeta (to taste)

Instructions:

1. Preheat oven to 400 degrees.

2. Wash the cauliflower and slice into ¼" to ½" slices, then place in a large bowl. Add enough olive oil to lightly coat all of the cauliflower, add Vegeta as desired.

3. Toss gently.

4. Arrange the cauliflower in one layer, on a baking sheet lined with parchment.

5. Bake at 400 degrees for 30 minutes, or until cauliflower is tender and beginning to brown on the edges. Enjoy!

CHEF BABA TIP: You can also add other spices, such as red pepper, or red paprika (sweet or hot) before baking.

Damir cuts into ¼" to ½" slices.

Adds olive oil to coat all of the cauliflower.

Baba arranges the cauliflower in one layer.

She places the cauliflower on parchment.

Baba bakes it for 30 minutes, or until cauliflower is tender and beginning to brown on the edges.

Baba's Oven-Roasted Brussel Sprouts

These tasty brussel sprouts go nicely with any of Baba's pork dishes.

- Season 5
- Preparation Time: 15 minutes
- Baking time: 30 minutes
- Serves: 4 to 6

Ingredients:

1 pound fresh Brussel sprouts
2 to 3 tablespoons olive oil
1 tablespoon Vegeta (or salt)
1 teaspoon black pepper
Optional: sweet red paprika

Damir trims off the ends and any yellow leaves.

Damir cuts the sprouts in half.

Instructions:

1. Preheat oven to 400 degrees.

2. Wash the Brussel sprouts. Trim off the ends and any yellow leaves, then cut in half lengthwise. Place in a large bowl. Add enough olive oil to lightly coat all of the sprouts, and add vegeta and pepper, or other spices as desired. Toss gently. Arrange the sprouts in one layer, on a baking sheet lined with parchment.

Baba adds enough olive oil to lightly coat all of the sprouts, and adds Vegeta and pepper, or other spices as desired.

3. Bake at 400 degrees for 30 minutes, or until the sprouts are tender and beginning to brown. Enjoy!

CHEF BABA TIP: For extra flavor, toss with a little balsamic vinegar and honey after baking.

She bakes at 400 degrees for 30 minutes, or until the sprouts are tender and beginning to brown.

Baba's Mashed Sweet Potatoes

A healthy version of sweet potatoes that can be served anytime, and a must for Thanksgiving dinner in America.

- Season 5
- Preparation Time: 10 minutes
- Cooking Time: 30 to 45 minutes
- Serves: 8 to 10

Ingredients:

4 large sweet potatoes
Optional: butter, cinnamon

Instructions:

1. Preheat the oven to 400 degrees.

2. Wash the potatoes and poke with a fork several times, to release steam from the potatoes as they cook and keep them from bursting.

3. Wrap each potato in foil, and bake for 30 to 45 minutes. Remove from oven when the potatoes are tender when poked with a fork.

4. Remove the foil. Allow to cool slightly, then remove the potato skins while still hot. Mash with a potato masher. Enjoy!

CHEF BABA TIP: Baba serves her mashed sweet potatoes plain, but they are also delicious with a little butter and cinnamon.

Mashed sweet potatoes and Ajvar are a perfect side dish for baked trout.

Baba's Oven-Roasted Potato Wedges

These crunchy potato wedges are gone before anything else when they are on the dinner table. Nobody in Baba's family ever wants to share them.

- Season 4: Episode 6
- Preparation Time: 15 minutes
- Cooking Time: 45 minutes
- Serves: 4 to 6

Ingredients:

> 4 or 5 large russet potatoes
> 1 ½ to 2 cups sunflower oil
> 2 tablespoons Vegeta

Instructions:

1. Cut each potato into 6 length-wise wedges, ½" to 1" thick. Pat the potatoes dry with a paper towel. Toss with 2 tablespoons of sunflower oil and Vegeta seasoning.

2. Pour sunflower oil into a baking pan to about ½" deep. Place the pan in the oven and preheat to 375 degrees. When oven is preheated, remove pan of oil and add the potatoes to the pan.

3. Bake the potatoes for about 20 minutes, or until they are tender. Remove from the oven, toss with a spatula. Continue baking until the edges are brown and crispy.

4. Watch as these potatoes disappear quickly.

Baba admires her crunchy potato wedges, fully knowing they will be gone within minutes.

Baba's Glazed Carrots

The tender carrots in a rich, buttery apricot sauce are special indeed. They are a great side to pork, beef or chicken.

- Season 5
- Preparation Time: 10 minutes
- Cooking Time: 30 minutes

Ingredients:

1 pound whole, fresh carrots
1 ½ teaspoons salt
2 tablespoons butter
2 tablespoons sugar
½ cup apricot preserves

Peel the carrots and slice length-wise. Place them in boiling water. Add a teaspoon of salt. Cover and cook for about 10 minutes.

Instructions:

1. Peel the carrots and slice length-wise. Place them in boiling water. Add a teaspoon of salt. Cover and cook for about 10 minutes, or until they are a little tender. Drain off the water. Cut the carrots in half.

2. Place the butter and sugar in a small skillet. Mix over high heat until the sugar is dissolved into the butter, about 1 minute. Add the apricot preserves and mix until smooth. Add ½ teaspoon of salt. Add the carrots and toss to coat. Lower heat and simmer carrots to desired tenderness.

3. Serve hot.

Baba's Glazed Carrots complement Beef Wellington and oven-roasted potatoes beautifully.

We had a huge garden on our farm in Yugoslavia. My husband Ivan and I were organic before "organic" was fashionable. We grew onions, tomatoes, spinach, cabbage, lettuce, and a lot of potatoes. Today, we would be considered super-hip with the urban crowd because we grew our own vegetables, plus raised chickens and pigs. When it came to potatoes, my children loved when I roasted them in the oven, or made potato biscuits.

When my twin boys started first grade, Damir did not like school. He complained about it all the time. It took a lot of Serbian screaming to make him go to school. Finally, after many days of Damir's complaining, his father took another approach. Arriving home from school, Damir found his father working in the garden, taking the potatoes out of the ground with a pitchfork. He was careful not to ruin the plant.

"I don't want to go to school anymore, Tata," Damir announced.

His father kept working the garden. Finally, Ivan stopped working and told Damir, "Okay. You don't have to do it anymore. You can just stay on the farm and work the garden and the cornfields."

"When can I start?" Damir asked excitedly.

"You can start now. I need you to help me get the potatoes out."

And for the next few hours, Damir worked diligently with his father getting the potatoes out of the ground. It was hard work and Ivan did not give him a break. They were halfway done and Damir could see that there was so much more to do.

"Tata, I think I want to go to school instead," Damir said as Ivan dug in the pitchfork so that Damir could pick up the potatoes.

"Dobro, Damire," Ivan said. You can go and play with your brother now.

Damir ran away from the garden as fast as a little rat.

I have many fond memories of growing all kinds of produce in our large garden. It was hard work but extremely satisfying because growing plants of any kind always warms my heart.

Working in a garden is therapeutic. It soothes the body, spirit and soul. Working the potatoes in the garden had a huge effect on Damir. He worked hard on the farm but he realized at a very young age that without education, there is no future. Today, he is a huge bookworm and an avid student of many topics. And he is also a huge fan of my roasted potatoes, apricot dumplings and potato-based Šufnudle.

— Love, Chef Baba

Šufnudle (Potato Dumplings)

In America, they are called potato dumplings. This dough recipe can also be used for Potato Biscuits or to wrap Plum and Apricot Dumplings.

- Season 2: Episode 8
- Serves: 8 to 10
- Total Time to Make: 1 ½ hours

Ingredients:

7 large potatoes
1 pinch of salt
¼ cup plus 2 tablespoons olive oil
2 eggs
All-purpose flour (enough to
    make ⅓ ratio to ⅔ potatoes)
1 handful plain bread crumbs

Instructions:

1. Place the whole potatoes, leaving on the skins, in a large pot. Cover completely with water. Cover with a lid and heat over high heat until boiling. Continue boiling about 4 minutes, or until the potatoes are tender when poked with a fork.

2. Remove the potatoes from the heat. Strain off the water. Allow the potatoes to cool about 5 minutes. While the potatoes are still hot, carefully remove the skins by holding a potato in one hand, using a folded paper towel to keep from burning your hand. With your other hand, use a knife to peel the potato skin off in strips.

3. Place the potatoes in a large mixing bowl. Allow to cool.

4. Mash the potatoes using a potato masher. Add salt, 1 tablespoon of olive oil and two eggs. Add enough flour to make a 1/3 ratio of flour to 2/3 of potatoes. Mix the dough with your hands.

5. Lightly flour your work surface. Place the dough on the surface and knead it until smooth. Sprinkle flour on the work surface as needed to keep the dough from sticking.

6. Fill a large pot ½ full of water. Add 1 tablespoon of olive oil. Bring to a boil.

7. Roll the dough into finger-thick strips. Cut into 3" long pieces. Drop the dough pieces, one-by-one into the boiling water. Gently stir occasionally. When the pieces rise, after about 15 minutes, drain the noodles and place them in a large baking dish.

8. Heat ¼ cup of olive oil in a small skillet. Add the breadcrumbs and stir. Cook until light brown. Pour the breadcrumb mixture over the noodles. Mix gently until the noodles are evenly coated.

9. Bake at 350 for 15 to 20 minutes. Serve hot.

Baba places the whole potatoes in a large pot. She covers them with water and a lid. Heats until boiling. She continues boiling for about 4 minutes, or until the potatoes are tender when poked with a fork. Baba removes from heat and drains the water. Allows the potatoes to cool for about 5 minutes.

While the potatoes are still hot, she carefully removes the skins by holding a potato in one hand, using a folded paper towel to keep from burning your hand. With her other hand, she uses a knife to peel the potato skin off in strips. Baba shows Danijela how to mash the potatoes using a potato masher while Damir supervises. Danijela adds salt, 1 tablespoon of olive oil and two eggs. She adds enough flour to make a ⅓ ratio of flour to ⅔ of potatoes.

Baba places the dough on the surface and kneads it until smooth. Sprinkles flour on the work surface as needed to keep the dough from sticking. Baba rolls the dough into finger-thick strips and cuts it into 3" long pieces.

Baba fills a large pot ½ full of water as Danijela and Luka observe. She adds 1 tablespoon of olive oil and brings it to a boil. Drops the dough pieces one-by-one into the boiling water. When the pieces rise, after about 15 minutes, she drains the noodles and places them in a large baking dish.

Baba heats ¼ cup of olive oil in a small skillet. She adds the breadcrumbs and stirs. Cooks until light brown. She pours the breadcrumb mixture over the noodles and mixes gently until noodles are coated.

Šufnudle (Potato Dumplings)   163

Desserts

The moral judgement of some of Chef Baba's family members becomes extremely clouded when it comes to eating incredible delights such as Krempita, Vasina Torta, Keks Torta or Vanilice—where they have to resort to trickery, manipulation and outright stealing to get to them first. And we're not even including Ivan, Chef Baba's grandson, in this highly competitive, dessert eating environment.

After my dad died, we had a family and friends gathering at Chef Baba's house to celebrate his life. There must have been 30 to 40 guests.

One of my father's friends wanted to attend the celebration but, because she was almost ninety years old, she needed someone to bring her to the house. I volunteered to pick her up just as the party began. I should have known better.

When we got to the house, the party was already in full swing. Some of my favorite Chef Baba dishes had already disappeared. The Gibanica was gone. The meat crepes were non-existent. The Vanilice were absent from the plates. Chef Baba had made a lot of food for the occasion but it was consumed at an unprecedented rate.

I went to the kitchen to see what was left over from the consumption carnage. Almost all of the other cookies were ab-sent too. To put it bluntly, nearly everything had been eaten.

As I stood there horrified, my then 17-year-old daughter Paige strolled up to me, smiling. She motioned quietly for me to step aside to the kitchen corner.

"Hey Dad, I did something cheesy. I took some of the Vanilice cookies and saved them for you. I know how much you love them," she said proudly.

She took me to one of the bedrooms, and laying on the bed covered with a kitchen towel were at least 20 cookies.

"Wow, you saved a lot of cookies, Paige," I said.

"Do you want me to take some of them back?" she asked.

I hesitated for a second, "No, we keep this for us. They've had more than enough. Thanks, Paige. You're my hero."

—Love, Damir

"Chef Baba's Sous Chef"

Vanilice

Chef Baba calls them Točkići or in English, Chef Baba's Little Wheel Cookies. These are delicate sugar cookies with a layer of apricot or your choice of fruit preserves inside. Baba's grandchildren eat these so fast she makes two batches and hides one batch for later. These cookies are easy to make and kids will enjoy helping make them too.

- Season 1: Episode 4
- Preparation time: 35 to 40 minutes
- Baking Time: 15 – 20 minutes / tray
- Serves 10-12

Ingredients:

6 cups flour (Baba uses King
 Arthur All Purpose flour)
1 cup granulated sugar
1 ¾ cups Crisco shortening
2 eggs
1 tablespoon Šljivovica (plum
 brandy or other liquor)
1 handful ground pecans or walnuts
5 tablespoons whole milk (or more)
Apricot preserves

Vanilice are the absolute perfect complement when drinking coffee—that is if you are lucky to have any of them left before Ivan gets a hold of them.

Instructions:

1. Preheat oven to 350 degrees.

2. Mix all of the ingredients, except for the preserves, in a large mixing bowl, using your hands. Form a large ball of dough and kneed until smooth. Cut into quarters and form 4 balls of dough.

3. Roll the balls of dough, one at a time, into large tube shapes, using your hands.

Roll the dough with a rolling pin, into an even layer about 1 finger thick. Cut with 1 inch to 2 inch circles using a cookie or biscuit cutter. Place on a large cookie sheet about ½ apart.

4. Bake at 350 for 15 minutes. (Varies by oven.)

Baba teaches Matthew Weldehiwot to mix all of the ingredients in a large mixing bowl, using his hands. Matthew forms a large ball of dough, cuts it into quarters and forms 4 balls of dough.

Baba teaches Matthew to roll the balls of dough into large tube shapes. Then she rolls the dough with a rolling pin, into an even layer about 1 finger thick.

Damir cuts 1 inch to 2 inch circles using biscuit cutter. He place them on a large cookie sheet about ½" apart.

Damir tells Baba that Matthew would make a great Chef Baba Sous Chef and this is an opportunity for Damir to retire.

Matthew tells Baba that he loves to cook.

Baba loves children that are interested in cooking. She wishes her children had the desire to learn to cook when they were young.

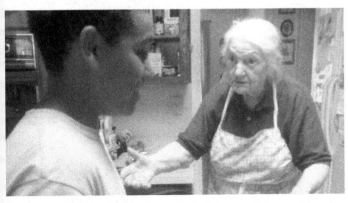

Baba tells Matthew that the secret to cooking is "simple cooking."

Baba asks Matthew to help Damir learn how to make Vanilice since he seems to be doing a better job.

Matthew, Baba and Damir pose after an extremely successful run of baking more than hundred Vanilice cookies in less then two hours.

Simply delicious. Perfect at any time, especially with coffee or cappuccino.

Chef Baba making Krempita late at night, before Thanksgiving 2017.

This is the confession of a Krempita thief and this person may need to be forgiven by Chef Baba—although I think she already knows the person behind the disappearance of this incredible dessert. It was the person without a nickname or country.

Chef Baba had three children, Jelena (Helen), Dejan (Danny) and Damir. You might have noticed—I don't know why but I never got a nickname in America. Oops. I just revealed who the Krempita thief was all these years. Yes, it was me—Damir—a guy without a nickname and according to my passport, a man without a country.* I stole Krempita—like all the time.

There is something about Krempita that completely clouds my moral fiber about sharing with others. I just can't resist. I have to satisfy my taste buds. Just

writing this story about Krempita makes my mouth salivate.

But if you have watched any of the Chef Baba episodes, you might think I say that about all of Chef Baba's desserts. Yes, I love them all, but Krempita holds a special place in my heart. This recipe, if you have never had it, is an absolute must for you to make … and enjoy. I am not sure I can do it any justice in describing how good it tastes. I love the rich vanilla filling supported by the delicate crust.

Krempita melts in your mouth. And the longer you keep it in the fringe (cool it for at least 24-48 hours), the better it tastes.

And cooling the Krempita overnight was where the idea of stealing began. The process of leaving it in the fridge is where I recognized the opportunity.

170 CHEFBABA COOKBOOK

After Chef Baba made Krempita, I would wait until late at night to become a raccoon-esque type of night prowler. I would quietly sneak, ninja-style into the garage—where Chef Baba kept her large, second refrigerator. I would carefully cut off a piece or two along the crusty edges of this incredible scrumptious dessert, and eat them.

Now, you would think that I would have gotten caught doing this because I'm famous for eating the edges of her Gibanica and Keks Torta, but luckily for me, my sister Helen also loved the corners of Krempita. This is most likely why my moral fiber went astray. I was in a race to beat Helen to those delightful edges of Krempita. And over the years, it has gotten worse.

We have new competition. Luka, Danny's son and my son Isaac have become Krempita frenemies as well. I can only predict the dessert thievery becoming more competitive. A few weeks before writing this chapter, Luka and Isaac beat me to the Krempita. They ate it all. I was a day late—which symbolizes the classic phrase, "You snooze, you lose." I now have a plan to begin making Krempita in my own home and enjoying it all to myself.

Baba, I hope you forgive me but I have finally come clean. But you better watch for others now too.

—Love, Damir
"Chef Baba's Sous Chef"

* During the Yugoslavian civil war, Americans refused to recognize Yugoslavia as a country and so when I updated my American passport to visit Europe, they stated as my country of origin, Sremska Mitrovica, which is my hometown.

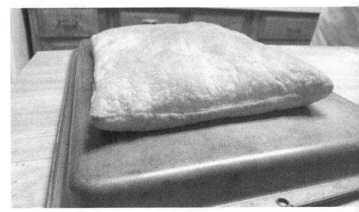
Krempita pastry cooling after being baked for 20 minutes.

Damir is thinking about stealing and eating all of Krempita himself the night of Thanksgiving 2017.

Baba catches him trying to steal Krempita and threatens to spank him with a wooden spoon.

Krempita

The most devoured of all of Chef Baba's desserts in the least amount of time.

- Season 2: Episode 7
- Total Time to Make: 1 to 2 hours
- Serves 8 to 10

Ingredients:

Frozen puff pastry sheet
  (Pepperidge Farm or from your
  local European grocery store)
6 eggs
12 tablespoons granulated sugar
4 cups whole milk
8 heaping tablespoons
  all-purpose flour
2 heaping tablespoons corn starch
2 packets vanilla sugar
Powdered sugar

Instructions:

1. Place the frozen pastry sheet on a lightly floured surface. Lightly flour the top of the pastry. Allow it to thaw for about 20 minutes.

2. Preheat oven to 375 degrees.

3. Turn a cookie sheet upside down and spray the bottom-side with cooking spray and lightly flour.

4. When pastry sheet is thawed, brush off any excess flour with a pastry brush.

5. Place the pastry sheet on the upside-down cookie sheet. Bake at 375 degrees until golden brown, about 20 minutes.

6. Remove the pastry crust from the oven. Allow to cool for 5 minutes. With a large bread knife, cut the crust in half so you have a top crust and a bottom. Open the halves and allow to cool.

7. To make the cream filling, separate the six eggs, placing the yolks in one medium sauce pan and the whites in another. Add the granulated sugar to the yolks and mix with a spatula until smooth.

8. Place the flour and cornstarch in a small bowl. Gradually add ⅓ to ½ cup of the milk as you stir with a spoon. Mix for a few minutes until well-blended.

9. Gradually add the remaining milk to the yolk mixture. Place it in a double boiler and heat at medium high. Add the vanilla sugar. Stir continuously until it begins to boil. Add the flour and corn starch mixture, pouring it through a strainer to remove any clumps. Continue stirring until it thickens and begins to boil. Remove from heat.

10. Beat the egg whites using an electric mixer on medium speed, then on high, until fluffy. Fold the eggs whites into the cream mixture, using a spatula. Blend with an electric mixer on low until smooth.

11. Place the pan of cream filling in the freezer overnight, or for at least 2 hours. Remove from the freezer.

CHEF BABA TIP: Do not stir.

12. Spread the cream filling evenly over the bottom of the pastry crust. Carefully place the pastry top over it.

13. Sprinkle with powdered sugar. Cut into squares, refrigerate for 24 hours. Serve.

Baba places the frozen pastry sheet on a lightly floured surface. Lightly flours the top of the pastry. She allows it to thaw for about 20 minutes.

To make the filling, Danijela separates the six eggs, placing the yolks in one medium sauce pan and the whites in another.

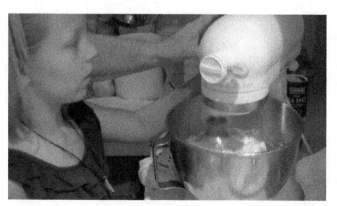

Baba shows Danijela and Damir how to mix the egg whites.

Damir adds 6 tablespoons of the granulated sugar to the yolks and mixes with a spatula until smooth.

Baba beats the egg whites using an electric mixer on medium speed, then on high, until fluffy. She folds the eggs whites into the cream mixture, using a spatula. Blends with an electric mixer on low until smooth.

After placing the pastry sheet on the upside-down cookie sheet, Baba bakes at 375 degrees until golden brown, about 20 minutes. Damir takes the pastry out of the oven.

After taking the pastry out of the oven, Damir accidentally tips over one of the pastry and almost ruins the episode. Luckily, he caught it.

Baba jumps on Damir for not paying attention during the process while Damir laughs.

Baba teaches Damir to use a large spoon. He spreads the cream filling evenly over the bottom of the pastry crust. Carefully places the pastry top over it.

Baba, Danijela and Damir enjoy the fruits of their labor. Luckily, Damir caught the pastry just in time or it would have been a Krempita-less day.

Baklava

Delicate layers of filo dough with a filling of ground pecans, drenched in a sweet syrup. Baba's rich, yet simple baklava simply melts in your mouth.

- Season 4: Episode 1
- Preparation Time: 30 minutes
- Cooking Time: 25 to 30 minutes
- Makes about 30 portions

Ingredients:

2 cups ground pecans
1 ¾ cup sunflower oil
3 ½ cup sparkling water (or club soda)
2 cups granulated sugar (Baba prefers King Arthur Sugar)
1 package (1 lb.) filo dough (Baba prefers Apollo Fillo Dough, No. 7)
Juice of 1 lemon

Instructions:

1. Allow the box of filo dough to thaw for at least 2 hours at room temperature, or minimum 3 hours in the refrigerator.

2. Preheat oven to 350 degrees. Brush cooking oil inside the bottom and sides of a 15" x 12" x 2" aluminum pan.

3. Roll out the filo dough onto a kitchen towel covered with the plastic sheet that came with the dough. Keep the filo dough covered with a towel as you are working, in order to keep it from drying out.

4. Place 2 sheets of dough on the bottom of the pan, spreading evenly.

5. Combine 1 cup of sunflower oil and 1 ½ sparkling water in a bowl. Use a pastry brush to evenly coat the top sheet of dough in the pan, with the water-oil mixture.

6. Place 2 sheets of dough on top and brush with the water-oil mixture. Sprinkle with a handful of ground pecans to form a thin, even layer. Sprinkle with a thin layer of sugar. Repeat the process, adding 2 sheets of dough at a time, then the pecans and sugar until you are have used all of the sheets of dough. Brush the top layer with the water-oil mixture.

7. Cut into diamond or square shapes all the way to the bottom of the pan.

8. Heat ¾ cup of oil in a small pan over medium heat. With a tablespoon, carefully drizzle the hot oil along the cut lines of the dough until you have used all of the oil.

9. Bake for 25 to 30 minutes. It will be done when it smells delicious and is golden brown and crispy.

Make the syrup:

1. While the Baklava is baking, combine 2 cups of sparkling water and 1 cup of sugar in a sauce pan. Bring to a full boil. Strain the lemon juice and add into the pan. Give it a quick stir and remove from heat. Allow to cool. Then place in the freezer until cold.

2. Pour the cold syrup over the hot baklava. Let it set for at least 30 minutes so the syrup is absorbed by the dough.

CHEF BABA TIP: You must either add cold syrup to hot Baklava, or add hot syrup to cold Baklava.

Baba allows the box of filo dough to thaw for at least 2 hours at room temperature, or minimum 3 hours in the refrigerator.

Baba brushes cooking oil inside the bottom and sides of a 15" x 12" x 2" aluminum pan while Damir and Ivan observe.

Baba rolls out the filo dough onto a kitchen towel covered with the plastic sheet that came with the dough. Keeps the filo dough covered with a towel as she works, in order to keep it from drying out.

Baba places 2 sheets of dough on the bottom of the pan. Adds, 1 cup of sunflower oil and 1 ½ cup of sparkling water. Mixes. Uses a brush to evenly coat the top sheet of dough in the pan, with the water-oil mixture.

She places 2 sheets of dough on top and brushes with the water-oil mixture. Sprinkles with a handful of ground pecans to form a thin, even layer.

Baba adds a thin layer of sugar. Repeats the process, adding 2 sheets of dough at a time, then the pecans and sugar until she has used all of the sheets of dough. Brushes the top layer with the water-oil mixture.

Using a sharp knife, Baba cuts the unbaked Baklava into diamond or square shapes.

She heats ¾ cup of oil in a small pan over medium heat.

With a tablespoon, she carefully drizzles the hot oil along the cut lines of the dough until she has used all of the oil.

Baba places it in oven for 25 to 30 minutes. It will be done when it smells delicious and is golden brown and crispy.

While the Baklava is baking, she combines 2 cups of sparkling water and one cup of sugar in a saucepan. She brings it to a full boil.

Baba allows the syrup to cool. Then she places it in the freezer until cold. Later, she pours the cold syrup over the hot baklava. Lets it set for at least 30 minutes so the syrup is absorbed by the dough.

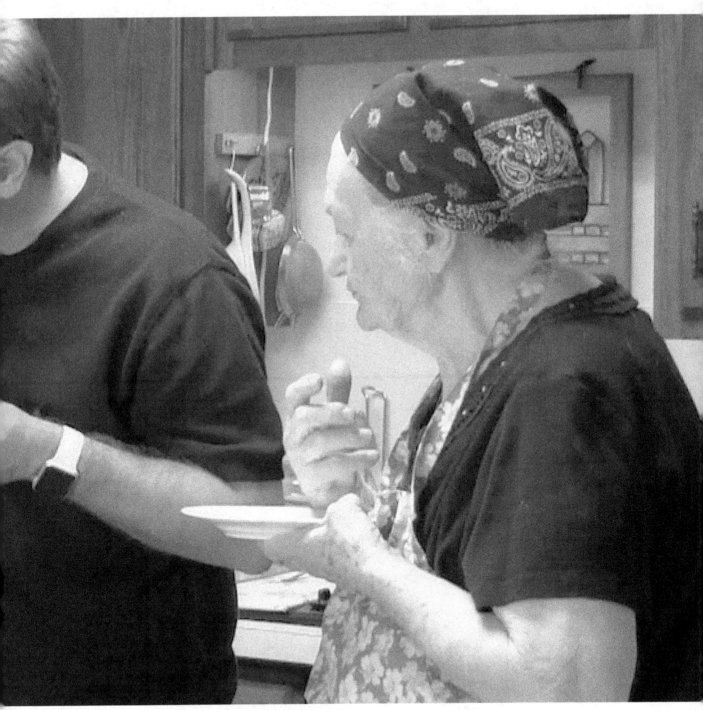

Chef Baba Tip: You must either add cold syrup to hot Baklava,
or add hot syrup to cold Baklava.

Vasina Torta

This is Baba's most special and most complicated cake recipe. It is worth the effort. A chocolate orange cake made with nuts and a layer of dark chocolate, then smothered in a delicious white icing.

- Season 3: Episode 7
- Preparation time: 2 hours
- Cooking Time: 1 hour
- Serves 10-15

Cake Layer Ingredients:

Zest of 1 large orange
10 eggs, separated
10 heaping tablespoons
    granulated sugar
10 heaping tablespoons
    ground almond
2 heaping tablespoons
    all-purpose flour
Cooking oil spray (Baba uses
    Pam cooking spray)

Instructions:

1. Preheat the oven to 350 degrees. Grate the orange peel from one large orange and place in a small bowl. Set aside. Separate the eggs, dividing the whites and the yolks into two large mixing bowls.

2. Mix the egg whites with an electric mixer until soft peaks.

3. Add sugar to the egg yolks and mix with an electric mixer on high, until smooth. Add the ground almond, flour and orange zest. Stir gently with a wooden stick or large spoon. Gradually fold in the egg whites, adding one large spoonful at a time and mixing gently.

4. Line a 10" round cake pan with parchment paper and lightly spray with cooking oil. Pour the batter into the pan. Smooth the top of the batter so it is even.

5. Bake at 350 degrees for 35 minutes. Do not open the door. While the cake is in the oven, make the chocolate-orange frosting as described below. When 35 minutes are up, turn off the oven and leave oven door closed for 5 minutes before removing the cake.

Chocolate-Orange Nut Ingredients:

Juice of 1 orange
4 eggs, separated
1 ⅔ stick butter
4 tablespoons sugar
¼ cup milk
1 ¼ cup ground pecans (or walnuts)
1 package (4.38 oz. /125 g.) 85%
    dark chocolate or baking
    chocolate
4 tablespoon powdered sugar

Chef Baba

Instructions for Chocolate-Orange Nut
Ingredients:

1. Juice the orange into a small bowl. Set aside. Separate the eggs and set aside.

2. Cut the butter into a pan. Add the sugar and milk. Heat over medium heat until the butter is melted, stirring frequently. When the butter is melted and the sugar dissolved, add the pecans. Continue stirring over medium heat until it thickens and you can see the bottom of the pan while mixing. Remove from heat and allow it to cool. Add the egg yolks and orange juice into the nut mixture. Stir well.

3. Melt the chocolate in the microwave, or in a shallow baking dish in the oven. Add the melted chocolate to the nut mixture. Mix thoroughly. Refrigerate until cool.

4. Remove the chocolate orange mixture from the refrigerator. Beat with an electric mixer, adding sugar if desired.

5. Spread the chocolate evenly in a thick layer over the top of the cake.

White Icing or Shaum Ingredients:

6 egg whites
1 cup granulated sugar
1 cup water

Instructions for White Icing or Shaum
Ingredients:

1. Combine the sugar and water in a large sauce pan. Heat on high, stirring frequently. Meanwhile beat the eggs whites to soft peaks. When the sugar boils and becomes thick and syrupy, place the pan in a larger pan of heated water, forming a double boiler. Continue stirring. Slowly add the egg whites, mixing well with a large spoon or wooden stick. Mix with an electric mixer on high, until fluffy.

2. Place the icing in the refrigerator to cool for 15 or 20 minutes. Spread evenly over the top and sides of the cake, reserving some of the frosting for decorating the cake later.

3. Refrigerate the cake and extra frosting overnight. Then next day, swirl the frosting around the sides of the cake. Dab extra frosting on top of the cake, creating swirls or floral shapes. Enjoy!

Baba lines a 10" round cake pan with parchment paper and lightly sprays with cooking oil. Pours the batter into the pan. She smooths the top of the batter so it is even. Bakes at 350 degrees for 35 minutes. (Do not open the door.)

Baba preheats the oven to 350 degrees. Damir separates the eggs, dividing the whites and the yolks into two large mixing bowls.

Damir grates the orange peel and places it in a small bowl. Sets it aside.

Damir separate the eggs into two large mixing bowls. Mixes the egg whites until soft peaks.

Baba adds sugar to the egg yolks and mixes with an electric mixer on high, until smooth. Adds the ground almond, flour and orange zest.

Baba juices the orange into a small bowl.

She cuts the butter into a pan. Adds the sugar and milk. Heats over medium heat until the butter is melted, stirring frequently. When the butter is melted and the sugar dissolved, she adds the pecans.

Damir continues stirring over medium heat until it thickens and he can see the bottom of the pan while mixing, allows it to cool. Adds the egg yolks and orange juice. Stirs well.

Baba adds the melted chocolate to the nut mixture. Mixes thoroughly. Refrigerates until cool.

Baba removes the chocolate orange mixture from the refrigerator. Damir beats it with an electric mixer, adding sugar if desired.

Baba spreads the chocolate evenly in a thick layer over the top of the cake.

She beats the eggs whites to soft peaks.

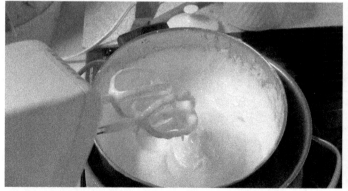

When the sugar boils and becomes thick and syrupy, Baba places the pan in a larger pan of heated water, forming a double boiler.

Damir continues stirring. Baba slowly adds the egg whites, mixing well with a large spoon or wooden stick. Mixes with an electric mixer on high, until fluffy.

Baba places the icing in the refrigerator to cool for 15 or 20 minutes. Spreads evenly over the top and sides of the cake, reserving some of the frosting for decorating the cake later.

Chef Baba refrigerates the cake and extra frosting overnight. Then next day, she swirls the frosting around the sides of the cake. Dabs extra frosting on top of the cake, creating swirls or floral shapes. Obviously, Damir is at it again. He's stealing the frosting and Baba is not very happy with him. Jon Dylan laughs seeing Baba scold his father.

188 CHEF   COOKBOOK

Kristen Homeyer, Jana Arnold and Chef Baba celebrate Baba's 84th birthday with Reforma Torta.

Reforma Torta

This is a rich, multi-layer cake with chocolate creme filling. It is a very delicious and special cake used for family celebrations like birthdays, weddings, Christmas and the New Year.

- Season 3: Episode 4
- Preparation time: 2 hours
- Cooking Time: 20 min
- Serves 12

CHEF BABA TIP: This recipe is for a two-layer cake. You can add additional layers by adding 6 eggs, plus half of the other ingredients, for each layer.

Walnut Sponge Cake Ingredients:

> Egg whites of 12 large eggs
> (set aside yolk to use for frosting)
> 1 cup granulated sugar
> 4 cup ground pecans or walnuts

Instructions:

1. Preheat the oven to 350 degrees.

2. Line two 10" to 12" cake pans with foil and spray lightly with cooking oil. Use one cake pan for each layer.

3. Separate the eggs. Place the yolks in a medium bowl and set aside for making the frosting (instructions below). Beat 6 egg whites on slow using an electric mixer or hand mixer until foamy, slowly adding ½ cup sugar. Gently fold 2 cups of the pecans or walnuts into the egg white mixture, adding a little at a time. Mix thoroughly, then transfer the batter into a cake pan, smoothing the top with a spatula to create an even layer.

4. Bake at 350 for 20 minutes, without opening the oven door.

5. While the first layer is cooking, repeat the recipe above, using the second half of the ingredients. Thoroughly clean the bowl before mixing the egg whites for the second cake layer.

6. Remove from the oven when the cake is golden. Allow to cool for 5 minutes, then turn over onto a serving plate to cool while you make the frosting.

Baba's Chocolate Frosting Ingredients:

> 12 egg yolks
> 4 tablespoons water
> 1 cup granulated sugar
> 1 (8-ounce) package baking
> chocolate
> 2 sticks of unsalted butter

Instructions:

1. Mix together the sugar and water to the egg yolks in a sauce pan (or use a

double boiler). Stir until mixed thoroughly. Place the sauce pan into a skillet with an inch of water, to create a double boiler. Turn heat to medium. Heat the egg mixture, stirring continuously. Add the baking chocolate piece by piece. Stir until the mixture thickens.

2. Remove from heat and add the butter piece by piece to the chocolate mixture. Mix with an electric mixer on low, then on high until the chocolate frosting is blended thoroughly and smooth.

3. Cool the chocolate frosting in the refrigerator until it is very thick (about 30 minutes). Mix again with an electric mixer until fluffy.

Assemble the Cake:

1. Spread half of the frosting on the sides and top of the first layer of cake. Place the second layer of cake on top and cover with the remaining frosting. Optional: Sprinkle with ground pecans and chocolate shavings.

2. Refrigerate the cake overnight before serving.

Damir separates the eggs. Places the yolks in a medium bowl and sets them aside for making the frosting.

Baba beats 6 egg whites on slow using an electric mixer or hand mixer until foamy, slowly adding ½ cup sugar.

She gently folds 2 cups of the pecans or walnuts into the egg white mixture, adding a little at a time. Mixes thoroughly.

Baba transfers the batter into a cake pan, smoothing the top with a spatula to create an even layer.

She bakes the cake at 350 for 20 minutes, without opening the oven door. While first layer is cooking, Baba repeats the recipe above, using the second half of the ingredients.

When the cake is golden, she removes from the oven. Allows it to cool for 5 minutes, then turns it over onto a serving plate to cool while she makes the frosting.

Baba adds the sugar and water to the egg yolks. Stirs until mixed thoroughly.

She places the sauce pan into a skillet with an inch of water, to create a double boiler. Heats the egg mixture, stirring continuously.

Baba adds the baking chocolate piece by piece. Stirs until the mixture thickens.

Adds the butter piece by piece to the chocolate mixture. Mixes with an electric mixer on low, then on high until the chocolate frosting is smooth.

Baba cools the chocolate frosting in the refrigerator until it is very thick (about 30 minutes). Mixes again with an electric mixer until fluffy.

Damir spreads half of frosting on the sides and top of the first layer of cake.

Baba places the second layer of cake on top of the frost.

Damir spreads the second half of the frosting on the sides and on top of the second layer of cake.

Baba and Damir inspect the beautiful chocolate frosting.

Baba sprinkles ground pecans all over the cake, then refrigerates it over night before serving.

Perfect cake for birthdays—including Chef Baba's birthday. Hopefully, she does not have to make her own birthday cake for her 84th birthday.

When my son Damir moved to Silicon Valley, I missed my grandchildren very much. For my granddaughter Paige's 8th birthday, I made Keks Torta, her favorite cake, and shipped it to her for overnight delivery. I paid an outrageous sixty dollars to ship it overnight and had to pack it in dry ice.

When the cake arrived at my granddaughter's house, her parents were at work. Paige was upstairs in her room playing with her Beanie Babies. Without informing her, Paige's older brother Jon Dylan and his neighborhood friends ripped open the package, and they obviously couldn't help but eat half of the cake.

But they were not the only ones eyeing the cake. After taking their share of the delicious torta, they left it on the kitchen counter and went off into the backyard to go swimming in the pool.

When Paige went downstairs to the kitchen, thirty minutes later, she was horrified to find that Zeke, their Alaskan Malamute-wolf dog, was finishing off the last of the cake. From what I heard, Paige was not very happy with Zeke or her brother Jon. Despite Zeke's mischievous act, she was afraid Zeke would get sick and die from eating the chocolate cake. Fortunately, the only thing that Zeke got for eating the cake was a huge smile on his face as he licked his chops with joy. It was not a great birthday for Mira Paige, but at least her dog Zeke experienced chocolate heaven.

— Love, Chef Baba

Keks Torta

This chocolate cake is a family favorite, so Baba prepares it for most birthdays and other special occasions. No baking required.

- Season 1: Episode 8
- Preparation time: 1 hour + 2 nights refrigeration
- Cooking Time:
- Serves 12

Chocolate Frosting Ingredients:

> 8 eggs
> 4 tablespoons water
> ½ cup sugar
> 8 semi-sweet baking chocolate pieces (Baker's Chocolate is best)
> 2 sticks unsalted butter (softened)
> 2 boxes of Keks Butter Cookies, or 20 Graham Crackers (one 14.4–ounce box)

Instructions to make the chocolate frosting:

1. Break the eggs into a medium saucepan. Add the water and sugar and stir with a fork until thoroughly mixed.

2. Set the pan in a large skillet of water to create a double boiler. Add the chocolate and heat over high, stirring constantly using a wooden spoon, for about 20 minutes. The frosting is done when it has thickened.

3. Remove the frosting from the heat, add butter and mix thoroughly using an electric mixer. Refrigerate the entire pan of frosting overnight.

4. Remove the frosting from the refrigerator. Mix with an electric mixer until fluffy.

Instructions to assemble the cake:

1. Line an 8' x 12' glass baking dish with foil.

2. Place one layer of Keks or Graham Crackers in a baking dish to create the first layer (2 cookies x 4 cookies, or 4 Graham Crackers x 5 Graham Crackers).

3. Spread a layer of frosting across the first layer of cookies. Add a second layer of cookies, then a layer of frosting. Continue adding layers until all cookies are used. You will have four layers.

4. Reserve enough frosting to frost the sides of the cake.

5. Drag the back of a fork across the top of the cake, in a cross-hatch pattern to add texture. Refrigerate for 24 hours and serve.

CHEF BABA TIP: This recipe makes 4 layers, but the cake can have as many layers as you like.

Paige is teaching her cooking imbecile dad how to break eggs correctly.

Baba argues with Damir because Damir loves to push her buttons for fun.

Chef Baba dips Keks quickly, one at a time, into a cup of cold milk.

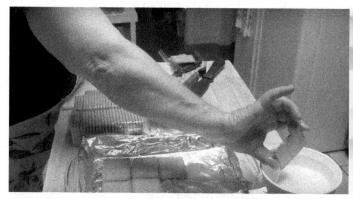

Damir observes Chef Baba spreading the frosting across the first layer of Keks. "This is not difficult, Baba," he states.

Chef Baba adds a second layer of Keks, then a layer of frosting until all Keks are used.

Chef Baba makes 4 layers, but the cake can have as many layers as you like. Reserve enough frosting to frost the sides of the cake.

One word to describe it: "Babalicious." The chocolate frosting is like pudding that it can be eaten with a spoon on its own.

Make sure you reserve enough frosting to frost sides of the cake. Drag the back of a fork across the top to add texture. Refrigerate for 24 hours.

Zeke Perge, an Alaskan Malamute, was a huge fan of Chef Baba. He's being taken for a walk by Paige.

Apricot Dumplings

Knedle sa Kajsija in Serbian. These large dumpling balls are made with whole apricots or plums. They are wrapped in a delicate potato dough and can be served as a main dish or a dessert. This potato dough is the same recipe Baba uses to make Šufnudle.

- Season 2: Episode 3
- Preparation time: 30 minutes
- Cooking Time: 45 minutes
- Makes 11 to 15 dumplings

Ingredients:

3 large russet potatoes (or 6 small potatoes)
11 to 14 apricots (or plums)
3 pinches of salt
2 eggs
2 cups all-purpose flour
2 tablespoons vegetable oil
1 handful plain breadcrumbs

Instructions:

1. Place the potatoes in a large pan. Cover with cold water. On the stove, heat at high until boiling. Reduce heat and continue boiling for about 30 minutes, or until the potatoes are soft when poked with a fork.

2. Drain the potatoes and allow them to cool. Carefully remove the skins.

CHEF BABA TIP: Don't burn your fingers. Use a folder paper towel to hold the hot potato in one hand, while carefully removing the skins with the other.

3. Mash the potatoes with a potato masher until there are no clumps. Set aside to cool.

4. Wash the apricots and remove the stems. Bring a large pot of water to boil, adding 1 pinch of salt.

5. Add 2 pinches of salt and the eggs to the mashed potatoes, mix. Add the flour and mix the dough with your hands.

6. Flour your work surface, and knead the dough until smooth. Form the dough into a ball. Using a rolling pin, roll the dough until it is about 1 inch thick. Cut the dough into squares about 3 or 4 inches, depending on size of fruit.

7. Place one apricot on a square of dough. Using your hands, wrap the dough around the apricot, then roll it between your hands until the dough is evenly spread all around the apricot. Add flour to your hands as needed to keep the dough from sticking. Wrap each piece of fruit with dough, in the same manner.

8. Add 1 tablespoon of vegetable oil to the boiling pot of water. Drop the dumplings into the pot. After about 15 minutes, they will rise to the top and are done.

9. While the dumplings are boiling, in a medium sauce pan, add 1 tablespoon of vegetable oil. Heat over medium. Add the breadcrumbs and stir.

10. Preheat oven to 375 degrees.

11. Remove the dumplings from the boiling water, with a slotted spoon. Place in a bowl of cold water to stop the cooking process. Remove the pan with the breadcrumb mixture from heat. One at a time, place the dumplings in the pan of breadcrumbs and roll around to coat evenly with breadcrumbs. Place the dumplings in one layer, in a large baking dish.

12. Bake the dumplings at 375 degrees for 15 min. Remove from oven and serve hot.

Damir drains the potatoes and allows them to cool. Carefully removes the skins. Mashes the potatoes with a potato masher until there are no clumps.

Baba adds 2 pinches of salt and the eggs to the mashed potatoes, mixes. Adds the flour and mixes the dough with her hands.

Baba places the potatoes in a large pan. Covers with cold water. On the stove, heats at high until boiling. Reduces heat and continues boiling for about 30 minutes.

Damir forms the dough into a ball. Using a rolling pin, rolls the dough until it is about 1 inch thick.

Damir and Baba wrap the dough around the apricot, then roll it between their hands until the dough is evenly spread all around the apricot.

Baba cuts the dough into squares about 3 or 4 inches, depending on whether she has larger or smaller fruit. Places one apricot on a square of dough.

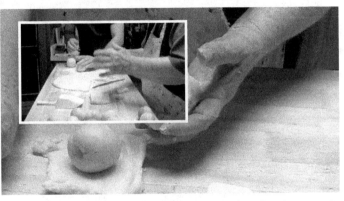

Using her hands, Baba wraps the dough around the apricot, then rolls it between her hands until the dough is evenly spread all around the apricot.

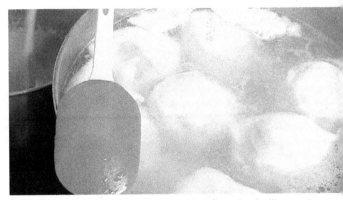

She adds 1 tablespoon of vegetable oil to the boiling pot of water. Drops the dumplings into the pot. After about 15 minutes, they will rise to the top and are done.

While the dumplings are boiling, in a medium sauce pan, Baba adds 1 tablespoon of vegetable oil. Heats over medium. Adds the breadcrumbs and stirs. Preheats oven to 375.

Baba places the dumplings in a bowl of cold water. Removes the pan with the mixture. Places each dumpling in the pan of breadcrumbs and rolls around to coat evenly. Bakes for 15 min.

In Yugoslavia we had a huge walnut tree in front of our farmhouse. Our farm was one kilometer from the train station and a fifteen-minute walk to the center of the city.

This gorgeous walnut tree was a centerpiece for many of our family gatherings in the spring, fall and summer. She produced incredibly large and delicious walnuts. My twin boys would climb so high up in that tree, against my wish-es, that I dare not yell at them as they were hanging from the branches like little monkeys, because I was afraid to startle them.

I made hundreds of Panama Tortas during those years in Yugoslavia. Using eggs from our own henhouse, and those beautiful walnuts, made this cake extra special for my family.

—Love, Chef Baba

Panama Torta

Baba also calls it Chocolate Walnut Cake. This traditional Eastern European cake is moist and light. The rich pudding-like chocolate frosting is so delicious you can eat it with a spoon. This cake can be made with your choice of pecans or walnuts.

- Season 1: Episode 2
- Preparation time: 3 to 3 ½ hours
- Baking Time: 42 minutes
- Serves 12

Frosting Ingredients:

8 eggs
4 tablespoons water
6 ounces granulated sugar
1 (8-ounce) package Baker's chocolate
2 sticks butter

Instructions to make the frosting:

1. In a large pot, mix the eggs, water and sugar. Place the pot in a skillet of water, creating a double boiler. Heat over medium high, stirring continuously. Add the chocolate, piece by piece. Continue stirring to melt the chocolate.

2. Bring the water to a boil, then lower the heat to medium. Continue stirring until the chocolate frosting is thick enough that you can see the bottom of the pot as you stir. Remove from the heat. Add the butter, piece by piece. Blend with electric mixer, on low speed, until smooth. Place the pot of frosting in the freezer for 1 hour to cool, or in the refrigerator for at least 2 hours.

Chocolate Walnut Cake Ingredients:

10 eggs, separated
6 ounces granulated sugar
2¾ cups ground walnuts or pecans
2 heaping teaspoons cocoa powder
4 heaping tablespoons all-purpose flour

Instructions to make the cake:

1. Preheat the oven to 375 degrees. Prepare a 10 ½" springform cake pan by lining it with parchment paper, and spraying lightly with cooking spray.

2. Separate the eggs, placing the egg whites in one large mixing bowl and the yolks in another.

3. Add the sugar to the yolks. Mix with an electric mixer at low speed, until smooth and all of the sugar has been dissolved, about 2 or 3 minutes. Mix the egg whites with an electric mixer on low speed, until thick and foamy (soft peaks).

4. Mix together the ground walnuts, cocoa powder and flour in a small bowl. Add the nut mix and egg whites into the egg yolk mixture. Gently fold everything together using a large spoon or spatula. Do not overmix.

5. Pour the batter into the cake pan. Smooth the top so it is even. Bake for 35 minutes. Do not open the oven door while cooking. After 35 minutes, simply turn off the oven and allow the cake to sit inside for 2 minutes before opening the oven door. Open oven door slightly, to allow heat to escape, and let the cake sit untouched in the oven for an additional 5 minutes.

6. Remove the cake from the oven. Grab the edges of the parchment paper to lift the cake out of the pan. Place it on a cooling rack. Gently pull the parchment paper away from the sides of cake. Allow to cool. After the chocolate frost-ing has set, remove from the refrigerator or freezer. Mix until fluffy, using an electric mixer on low speed.

7. Slide the cake off of the parchment paper, onto a cake plate. Use a large knife or cutting thread to cut the cake into 2 layers.

8. Smooth chocolate frosting gener-ously across the bottom layer. Place the top layer carefully over the bottom layer. Smooth frosting evenly over the top and sides of the cake. You may have frosting left over. Refrigerate the cake overnight before serving. Enjoy this cake cold.

Baba mixes the eggs, water and sugar in a large pot.

She places the pot in a skillet of water, creating a double boiler.

Baba heats it over medium high, stirring continuously.

When the water begins to boil, she lowers the heat to medium. Continues stirring until the chocolate frosting is thick enough to see the bottom.

To make the cake layer, Damir separates the eggs, placing the egg whites in one large mixing bowl and the yolks in another.

Damir adds the sugar to the yolks and mixes with an electric mixer at low speed.

Damir mixes the batter at low speed, until smooth and all of the sugar has been dissolved.

Damir mixes the egg whites with an electric mixer on low speed, until thick and foamy.

In a small bowl, he mixes together the ground walnuts cocoa powder and flour.

Baba takes over and adds the nut mix and egg whites into the egg yolk mixture. Gently folds everything.

Damir learns to gently fold everything together using a large spoon and makes sure not overmix.

Damir pours the batter into the cake pan and smooths the top so it is even.

Damir bakes for 35 minutes. Do not open the oven door while cooking.

After 35 minutes, she turns off the oven and allows the cake to sit inside for 2 minutes before opening the oven door. Opens the oven door slightly.

She removes the cake from oven. Places it on a cooling rack. Gently pulls the parchment paper away from the sides of cake.

Damir smooths chocolate frosting generously across the bottom layer.

Baba supervises Damir's spreading technique.

Baba smooths the frosting evenly over the top and sides of the cake. Sprinkles the ground nuts.

Living on a farm is so much fun. When my parents left for America, they gave the responsibility of taking care of the farm to my sisters and me. Joja (Jovanka) lived on the farm until she got married to Braca (Sergije Urukalo). After they moved to their apartment, Beba (Olivera) and Pera Radović grew wheat on the acreage across the road from us, while my husband Ivan and I grew mostly corn every year.

Working on the farm while also having full time jobs was no easy task. Ivan was a civil engineer and was responsible for bringing the water infrastructure to the small towns in the Srem region. After World War II, a substantial number of homes and farms were still without running water. In fact, we did not have inside plumbing until my twin boys were seven years old. It was Ivan who finally convinced city hall to bring the water infrastructure to our neighborhood. Ivan was like a rock star in our region. He was a former champion weightlifter of Yugoslavia, so was already kind of famous in

the region. But he became even more popular for bringing water to the kitchens and bathrooms of the area. When he brought water into our own kitchen, he enabled me to cook like a speed demon.

We upgraded the farm, year after year, with internal and external improvements. So the farm became an attraction point for all my sisters and friends to visit on the weekends. During the fall corn harvest, most of my sisters and brother-in-laws pitched in to help harvest the corn. As a token of huge appreciation, I cooked a lot of food during the harvest. I made apple and pumpkin strudels, from what we grew on the farm. It brought me great joy to make it for everyone. I have fond memories of the good times during those corn harvests. It was hard work and everyone worked hard—but we also knew how to celebrate afterwards through joyous conversations, great food and enough Šljivovica to keep everyone warm inside.

—Love, Chef Baba

Apple and Pumpkin Strudels

This is a perfect desert for fall. The smell of the apples and pumpkin baking just might make your neighbors flock to your house. This strudel is made with 3 or 4 sheets of filo dough and has a delicate, layered crust that is crispier than the crust of the Poppy Seed, Pecan and Apricot strudel recipe.

- Season 2: Episode 6
- Preparation time: 20 to 30 minutes
- Cooking Time: 30 minutes
- Makes six delicious strudels — 3 apple and 3 pumpkin

Ingredients:

> 3 wedges of fresh pumpkin
> 6 apples (Granny Smith,
>   Macintosh or Gala)
> Cooking spray
>   (Baba uses Pam cooking spray)
> 1 box filo dough (thawed)
> 2 cups vegetable oil
> 2 cups granulated sugar
> 3 teaspoons ground cinnamon
> 2 tablespoons club soda
>   (or sparkling water)

Instructions:

1. Using a large, sharp knife, slice a medium pumpkin into wedges, following the natural creases of the pumpkin. Scrape the interior seeds and pulp from 3 of the wedges, and carefully cut off the outside skin. (You can freeze the remaining pumpkin for later use.) Use a metal cheese grater to shred the pumpkin wedges, then place in a large mixing bowl.

2. Peel the apples and shred them with a metal cheese grater. Place the shredded apple in a separate large mixing bowl.

3. Spray a 10" x 15" cookie sheet with cooking spray.

4. Carefully unroll 1 package of filo dough (there are usually two packages per box). Lay the filo dough sheets on the plastic that it was wrapped in, and cover with a kitchen towel so the dough does not dry out while you are working. Carefully lay one filo dough sheet on a second kitchen cloth, and gently brush with vegetable oil. Place a second filo dough sheet on top of the first and brush with oil. Repeat until you have 4 filo dough sheets layered on top of each other. Do not brush oil on top layer—brush it with club soda.

5. By the handful, pick up the shredded apple and gently squeeze out excess juice. Arrange one third of the shredded apple in a 3 ½" wide strip along the long edge of the filo dough. Sprinkle about

¼ cup of sugar over the apple. Using a spoon, drizzle oil over the apple. Sprinkle the cinnamon and a little more sugar.

6. Roll the strudel, starting on the side with the apple and roll across creating a long roll. Place the strudel roll carefully on the cookie sheet. Repeat the process to make a second and third apple strudel. Brush the tops of the rolled apple strudels with oil.

7. Preheat oven to 375 degrees. Bake the apple strudel for 20 minutes or until golden brown. Cover with foil for last 5 minutes of cooking to keep the crust from being over cooked. Remove from oven and cover with paper towels. Serve hot or cold. If desired, sprinkle with powdered sugar before serving.

8. Prepare the pumpkin strudel while the apple strudel is in the oven. As before, layer 4 filo dough layers, brushing the first three with vegetable oil and the

forth with club soda. Add one third of the pumpkin to the top layer in a 3 ½" strip along the long side of the dough. Drizzle vegetable oil over the pumpkin. Sprinkle 2 or 3 tablespoons of sugar over the pumpkin. Sprinkle with cinnamon. Drizzle with a little more oil.

9. Spray a large cookie sheet with cooking oil. Roll the strudel, starting on the side with pumpkin and roll all the way. Place on the cookie sheet. Repeat the process two times to make three pumpkin strudels. Brush club soda on top of the strudels.

10. Bake the pumpkin strudels for 30 or so minutes at 375 until golden brown. Cover with foil for last 5 minutes of cooking to keep the crust from being over cooked. Remove from the oven and cover with paper towels. Serve hot or cold. If desired, sprinkle with powdered sugar before serving.

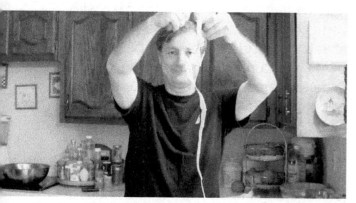

Damir peels the apple and plays with it like he used to as a child growing up in Yugoslavia.

He then grates the apples into a large bowl.

Baba carefully unrolls the filo dough from the package and, using 4 layers of filo dough, she places one layer at a time onto a cloth and gently brushes with oil.

Baba picks up the apple by the handful and squeezes out juice and places it a 3 ½" wide strip along the edge of the filo dough. Using spoon, she drizzle oil over the apples.

After she rolls the strudel, she brushes the top of the strudels with oil.

Baba preheats the oven to 375 degrees, and bakes the strudel for 20 minutes or until golden brown. She covers it with foil for the last 5 minutes of baking to keep from being overcooked.

After removing the strudels from the oven, Chef Baba covers them with paper towels and waits for them to cool. The dish can be served hot or cold. Damir prefers it hot.

Baba sprinkles the strudels with powdered sugar.

Apple and Pumpkin Strudels 209

Česnica

Česnica (Serbian Christmas Bread). This bread is traditionally served on Christmas Day in Serbia. The cook hides a coin inside the dough before baking. The person who finds the coin is granted good luck all year. In Chef Baba's house the coin is returned to the host of the party in exchange for $100 cash.

- Season 3: Episode 8
- Preparation Time: 10 minutes
- Cooking Time: 35 minutes
- Serves: 6 to 10

Ingredients:

1 package (1 lb.) filo dough, (Baba prefers Apollo Fillo Dough, No. 7)
1 cup cooking Oil (Baba uses sunflower oil)
1 ½ cups sparkling water (or club soda)
Honey

Instructions:

1. Allow the box of filo dough to thaw for about 2 hours at room temperature, or at least 3 hours in the refrigerator.

2. Preheat the oven to 375 degrees. Brush cooking oil inside the bottom and sides of a 15" x 12" x 2" aluminum pan.

3. Roll out the filo dough onto a kitchen towel covered with the plastic sheet that came with the dough. Keep the filo dough covered by a towel as you are working in order to keep it from drying out.

4. Place 3 sheets of dough on the bottom of the pan, spreading evenly. Fold the edge of the dough in along one side to fit the pan.

5. Mix the cooking oil with the sparkling water in a small bowl. Use a pastry brush to evenly coat the top layer of the filo dough in the pan, with the water-oil mixture.

6. Add 2 more sheets of dough, folding over the edge of the dough in, to fit the pan, on the opposite side from the previous layer. Coat with the water-oil mixture.

7. Repeat the process, adding 2 sheets of dough at a time and brushing with oil until you have 3 sheets remaining. Work quickly so the filo dough does not dry out. Add the final 3 sheets and coat thoroughly with the water-oil mixture.

CHEF BABA TIP: Add the coin about half way through adding the layers. Place it in a corner to make it harder to find after baking.

8. Bake at 375 degrees for 25 minutes, then check it. The Česnica will puff up while baking. When it is golden brown all over, remove from oven.

9. Drizzle plenty of honey over the top. Tear the Česnica or cut into pieces and enjoy while still warm.

Baba allows the box of filo dough to thaw for about 2 hours at room temperature, or at least 3 hours in the refrigerator.

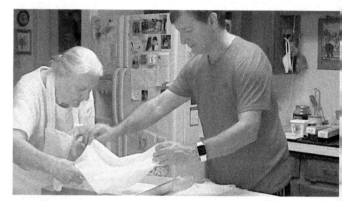

She preheats the oven to 375 degrees. Brushes cooking oil inside the bottom and sides of a 15" x 12" x 2" aluminum pan

Baba rolls out the filo dough onto a kitchen towel covered with the plastic sheet that came with the dough. Keep the filo dough covered by a towel to keep it from drying out.

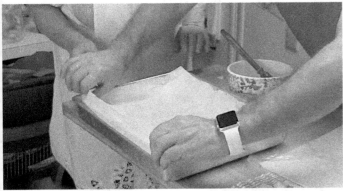

Damir places 3 sheets of dough on the bottom of the pan, spreading evenly. Folds the edge of the dough in along one side to fit the pan.

In a small bowl, Baba mixes the cooking oil with the sparkling water. She uses a pastry brush to evenly coat the top layer of the filo dough in the pan, with the water-oil mixture.

Baba bakes at 375 degrees for 25 minutes, then checks it. The Česnica will puff up while baking. She drizzles plenty of honey over the top.

Chef Baba Tip: Add the coin about half way through adding the layers. Place it in a corner to make it harder to find after baking.

Chef Baba was going to write about her European Apple Pie but I'm actually the authority on this recipe from a consumption perspective.

I have most likely had this dessert more often than any other dessert. As kids, my brother and I loved eating this pie after playing soccer for hours every day and would come home ravenous. This delicious pie is made with fresh apples and was simple for Baba to make any time we were begging for something sweet to give us energy.

You can eat this apple pie when it's really hot or when it's cold. In fact, if you put it in the refrigerator over night, it tastes magical the next day. I will admit that we almost never had leftovers.

European Apple Pie is absolutely magical.

—Love, Damir
"Chef Baba's Sous Chef"

Chef Baba

European Apple Pie

This delicious apple pie is simple to make and will disappear even faster than the time you took to make it.

- Season 2: Episode 1
- Preparation time: 1 hour
- Baking Time: 35 minutes
- Serves: 15

Ingredients:

10 apples (Granny Smith & Gala)
Juice of ½ lemon
4 4/5 cups all-purpose flour
¾ cup granulated sugar
2 sticks unsalted butter, softened
2 eggs
2 ounces while milk (add more
   if needed)
⅓ to ½ cup ground pecans
3 tablespoons granulated sugar

Instructions:

1. Peel the apples, then shred with a cheese grater. Place the shredded apples in a large bowl. Sprinkle lemon juice over the apples.

2. Combine the flour, sugar, butter, eggs and milk in a large mixing bowl. Mix thoroughly with your hands until mixed.

3. Place the dough onto a smooth surface. Add a few drops of milk if necessary, as you knead the dough until it is smooth, rolling gently. Divide into two

equal parts. Add more drops of milk if needed and roll into two long rolls of dough that are each the length of the 10" x 15" cookie sheet.

4. Preheat oven to 375 degrees.

5. Place one roll of dough on the cookie sheet and roll gently with a small rolling pin until the dough fits the entire cookie sheet.

6. To absorb extra juice during baking, sprinkle one half of the ground pecans over the dough on the cookie sheet.

7. To remove excess juice from the shredded apples, tilt the bowl of apples so the juice pools at side of the bowl. Spoon out the extra juice. Then grab the shredded apples, one handful at a time, and gently squeeze any excess juice into a bowl or cup.

8. Spread the shredded apples evenly over the dough on the cookie sheet. Sprinkle the 3 tablespoons of sugar, and the remaining pecans evenly over the apples.

European Apple Pie 215

CHEF BABA TIP: Yes, you can drink the excess fresh apple juice. Baba never wastes anything!

9. Sprinkle a little flour over your work surface. Using a rolling pin, roll the second roll of dough until it is an even layer, the size of the cookie sheet. Gently place the dough on top of the apples to form a top crust.

CHEF BABA TIP: To place the dough over the apples: roll the layer of dough gently around your rolling pin to pick it up, then unroll the dough across the shredded apples.

10. Stretch the dough to the edges of the pan by gently rolling it with a small rolling pin, or stretch it by hand. Puncture the dough several times with a fork in order to vent steam while cooking.

11. Bake for 35 minutes at 375 degrees. Add another 5 or 6 minutes if necessary to allow apple juice to evaporate. Bake until the crust is golden brown and crunchy. Sprinkle with powdered sugar and serve warm or cool.

Baba shows Damir how to peel the apples, then shreds them with a cheese grater. She places the shredded apples in a large bowl. Sprinkles lemon juice over the apples.

Damir removes excess juice from the shredded apples, tilts the bowl of apples so the juice pools at side of the bowl. Spoons out the extra juice.

Baba places the dough onto a smooth surface. Adds a few drops of milk if necessary, as she kneads the dough until it is smooth, rolling gently.

Baba spreads the shredded apples evenly over the dough on the cookie sheet. Sprinkles the 3 tablespoons of sugar, and the remaining pecans evenly over the apples.

Baba bakes the pie for 35 minutes at 375 degrees. Adds another 5 or 6 minutes if necessary to allow the apple juice to evaporate. She bakes until the crust is golden brown and crunchy.

Damir sprinkles powdered sugar and cuts the pie corners first for his own personal consumption. According to Damir, he's the official corner gatekeeper but the problem with his self-appointed position is that he ends up eating all the corners of the pie.

European Apple Pie   217

Chef Baba

Serbian Fruit Pie

Pita sa Višnjama in Serbian. This pie is delicious with fresh cherries, mixed berries, peaches or any fruit you want.

- Season 4: Episode 7
- Preparation Time: 15 minutes
- Cooking Time: 30 minutes
- Serves: 10 to 12

Ingredients:

1 pound fresh cherries, mixed
   berries or other fruit
2 eggs
¾ cup granulated sugar
1 packet vanilla sugar (or 1
   teaspoon vanilla extract)
½ cup vegetable oil
1 cup yogurt (plain or any flavor)
1 teaspoon light rum
1 teaspoon baking powder
2 cup all-purpose flour
1 handful granulated sugar
1 handful ground walnuts,
   pecans or almonds

Instructions:

1. Preheat the oven to 350 degrees

2. Whisk together the eggs, ½ cup of the granulated sugar, vanilla sugar, and vegetable oil. Add the yogurt and mix gently until smooth. Mix in the rum and lemon zest.

3. In a separate mixing bowl, combine the flour and baking powder. Mix. Add the dry ingredients to the wet ingredients. Mix until smooth.

4. Prepare a cake pan by lining with parchment paper and spraying lightly with cooking oil. Pour the batter into the cake pan. Bake for 10 minutes at 350 degrees.

5. Remove the partially-cooked batter from the oven. Mix the cherries or other fruit with ¼ cup of granulated sugar and the ground nuts. Carefully place the fruit evenly across the top of the batter, leaving a little space between each piece of fruit. Bake an additional 20 minutes at 350 degrees. Remove from the oven and enjoy! This pie is delicious hot or cold.

In a large bowl, Baba adds the eggs, ½ cup of the granulated sugar, vanilla sugar, and vegetable oil. She whisks to blend.

Baba adds the yogurt and mixes gently until smooth. Mixes in the rum and lemon zest.

Baba carefully places the fruit evenly across the top of the batter, leaving a little space between each piece of fruit.

Damir prepares a cake pan by lining with parchment paper and sprays lightly with cooking oil. Pours the batter into the cake pan. Bakes for 10 minutes at 350 degrees.

Baba pours the batter into the cake pan. She bakes for 10 minutes at 350 degrees.

Baba bakes an additional 20 minutes at 350 degrees. Removes the fruit pie from the oven.

Serbian Fruit Pie with berries.

Serbian Fruit Pie with cherries.

In the back, Oblatne and Voćna Salama.
Front row: Coconut Bars.

Chef Baba

Oblatne (Wafer Sheet Cookies)

Crunchy and sweet. These cookies have layers of rich chocolate cream and butter nut cream, sandwiched between crispy wafer sheets.

- Season 5
- Total Time to Make: 1 hour

Ingredients:

2 large wafer sheets
7 eggs
3 ½ cups powdered sugar
3 ⅔ cups graham cracker crumbs
4 to 6 dark chocolate squares,
  cut into thin slices
1 cup butter
2 to 3 packets vanilla sugar (or 2
  to 3 teaspoons of vanilla extract)
Juice of 1 lemon
A full handful of ground walnuts
or almonds

Instructions:

1. Separate the eggs into two medium mixing bowls.

2. To make the chocolate cream layer, beat the egg whites to stiff peaks, gradually adding 2 cups of the powdered sugar. Gently fold in the graham cracker crumbs and chocolate. Set aside.

3. Next make the butter nut layer. To the egg yolks, add 1 ⅔ cups of the powdered sugar, the butter, vanilla sugar,

Oblatne cookies are sweet delights.

lemon juice and ground nuts. Mix filling until smooth.

4. On a cookie sheet place one wafer sheet. Spread ½ of the chocolate evenly across the top. Add a layer of butter nut, then a layer of chocolate, and a final layer of butter nut.

5. Lay the second wafer sheet on top. Place a board, and a weight on top, to compress the layers for 24 hours. Remove the weight and cut the cookie into pieces, any shape you prefer. Enjoy.

CHEF BABA TIP: Oblatne cookies can be stored in the refrigerator in an air-tight container for two or three months.

Medena Pita (Honey Bars)

Everyone loves these delicate layered cookies with a thin layer of dark chocolate on top. These are Damir's favorite.

- Season 5
- Preparation Time: 60 minutes
- Cooking Time: 45 minutes

Cake Layer Ingredients:

4 cups all-purpose flour
¾ cup sugar
2 eggs
2 ½ tablespoons honey
½ cup milk
2 ½ tablespoons margarine or
   Crisco shortening
1 teaspoon baking powder

Medena Pita is one of Damir's favorite cookies.

Cake Layer Instructions:

1. Mix all ingredients together, with your hands, until smooth. Cut the dough into 4 equal pieces.

2. Turn a 10" x 15" baking sheet upside down, and spray the bottom with cooking oil, sprinkle with flour.

CHEF BABA TIP: To evenly flour the pan, sprinkle a 1" wide line of flour along one end of the pan. Tilt the floured end up, at a 45 degree angle, and tap the side of the pan. The flour will slide down the pan and leave an even layer.

3. Preheat oven to 350 degrees

4. Place a layer of dough evenly on the pan and bake for 10 minutes, until browned. Do not overcook. Bake all four cake layers and set aside.

Frosting Layer Ingredients:

3 ½ cup milk
6 tablespoons all-purpose flour
2 tablespoons gustine (or
   corn starch)
8 tablespoons sugar
2 sticks butter, softened

Instructions for Frosting Layer:

1. Mix ½ cup of the milk, the flour, gust-ine (or corn starch), and sugar in a small bowl. In a medium saucepan, heat the remainder of the milk. When the milk is hot, add the previous ingredients and stir well. Bring to a boil, stirring constantly, until the frosting is very thick. The frost-ing is done when, while stirring, you can see the bottom of the pan.

2. Remove from heat, cover and allow to cool completely. Mix the frosting with an electric mixer on high, until fluffy. Add the butter and mix on low until smooth. Set aside.

Chocolate Icing Ingredients:

⅔ package (100 g.) baking
    chocolate, (Bakers brand,
    semi-sweet is best)
3 to 4 tablespoons milk
1 teaspoon vegetable oil (Baba
    suggests safflower or
    sunflower oil)

Chocolate Icing Instructions:

1. Combine the chocolate, milk and vegetable oil in a small sauce pan. Heat over low until the chocolate is melted and the sauce is smooth.

Assemble the cake:

1. On a serving platter, place one layer of cake and spread ⅓ of the frosting on top. Add a second layer of cake, then ⅓ of the frosting. Add a third layer of cake, then the remainder of the frosting. Add the 4th layer of cake, then spread the chocolate icing evenly across the top, with a butter knife.

2. Refrigerate the cake for 24 hours. Then cut into bars or squares. These cookies can be kept in an air-tight con-tainer, in the refrigerator, for two or three months.

Madeleine, Ivan and Danijela focus on their cookies.

Medena Pita (Honey Bars) 225

Voćna Salama

Voćna Salama or No-Bake Date Cookies. Rich and Delicious.

- Preparation Time: 30 to 40 minutes, plus 6 hours refrigeration
- Makes: 36 cookies

Ingredients:

2 wafer sheets (11" x 9")
1 ⅓ cup (7 oz. or 200 g.) dried figs (Baba likes Krinos Kalamata Crown Figs from Greece)
1 ⅓ cup (7 oz. or 200 g.) dried plums
⅞ cup (2.5 oz. or 100 g.) pecans or walnut
2 tablespoons orange preserves
1 package (150 g.) keks wafer cookies
1 egg
1 egg yolk
⅔ cup (150 g.) sugar
⅔ cup (150 g.) butter
2 ¾ tablespoons (20 g.) cocoa powder
½ cup (50 g.) powdered sugar

Instructions:

1. To make the two wafer sheets flexible, lay them, side by side, between two damp kitchen towels. Set them aside until you are ready to use them.

2. Slice the dried figs and plums into thin strips. Chop the keks, cut into squares. Mix the figs, plums and keks together. Add the orange preserves and mix again.

3. Stir the egg and yolk together in a medium sauce pan. Stir in the sugar and butter. Add the cocoa powder. Set the pan in a larger pan of water, creating a double boiler. Heat over medium-high, stirring constantly. When the mixture thickens, remove from heat. Add this into the fruit mixture and stir until evenly mixed.

4. Sprinkle less than half of the powdered sugar on a cutting board. Place one softened wafer sheet on the powdered sugar. Spread half of the fruit mixture evenly across the wafer sheet, then roll tightly, along the short side of the wafer sheet. Add a little powdered sugar to the outside of the cookie roll, then roll it in foil so wrapped securely, and seal the ends. Repeat the process with the other wafer sheet. Refrigerate the cookie rolls for at least 6 hours. Slice into ½" cookies. Enjoy!

*Baba prefers Croatian wafer sheets from her local Eastern European store, such as Oblatne brand.

"I hope you have enjoyed my cookbook. Have fun cooking. And please remember, if Damir can learn how to cook, anybody can learn to cook."

Index

About Chef Baba Cooking Show

For further reference on the recipes in the Chef Baba Cookbook, please watch the episodes on chefbaba.com

Season 1	Season 2	Season 3	Season 4
S1: E1 Gibanica	S2: E1 European Apple Pie	S3: E1 Sarma & Stuffed Peppers	S4: E1 Pecan Baklava
S1: E2 Panama Torta	S2: E2 Krofne	S3: E2 Kiflice with Apricot Filling	S4: E2 Lepinjice
S1: E3 Meat Crepes	S2: E3 The Three Strudels	S3: E3 Pork Schnitzel	S4: E3 Pasulj & Prebranac
S1: E4 Vanilice	S2: E4 Apricot Dumplings	S3: E4 Reforma Torta	S4: E4 Baba's Chicken Chili
S1: E5 Chicken Noodle Soup	S2: E5 Listići	S3: E5 Pork Schnitzel	S4: E5 Pogača
S1: E6 Super-Thin Noodles	S2: E6 Apple & Pumpkin Strudels	S3: E6 Baba's Magic Salad	S4: E6 Lamb Chops & Potatoes
S1: E7 Russian Salad	S2: E7 Krempita	S3: E7 Vasina Torta	S4: E7 Serbian Fruit Pie
S1: E8 Keks Torta	S2: E8 Šufnudle & Potato Biscuits	S3: E8 Česnica	S4: E8 Ćevapčići

About the Authors

Miroslava "Chef Baba" Perge

Born in Yugoslavia, Miroslava Perge immigrated to the U.S. in 1974, at the age of 41, with her husband Ivan and three children. They left Yugoslavia because they could see the political and financial conditions changing. Without knowing one word of English, she built a new life with her family in a new country.

Now, at 85 years old, Miroslava has lived half of her life in Yugoslavia and half of it in America. Chef Baba has been cooking for seventy-five years and has not slowed down. Among family and friends, Chef Baba has always been known for her amazing cooking, particularly her Gibanica, chicken noodle soup, super-thin noodles, Lepinjice, Krempita, Listići, and ... well, actually the list goes on and on.

Miroslava learned to cook from her mother, who learned to cook from her mother and so on. She prepared those traditional Eastern European recipes so well that nobody else in the family wanted to cook. Why should they when Chef Baba could cook anything? After 15 years of Chef Baba telling her son Damir that she would not live forever—that's what Serbian Babas (grandmas) do—he finally got the message. Damir decided to shoot a video of Baba making his favorite recipe Gibanica. They had so much fun they started the *Chef Baba Cooking Show* on YouTube.

After numerous requests from Chef Baba's fans that she writes a cookbook, Damir has finally gotten off his smartphone to do something about it. Damir has taken on the responsibility of cataloging and recording all Chef Baba's recipes. Chef Baba has more than 600 recipes from the Old Country, so the sharing of her wonderful secret recipes continues.

For more information about Chef Baba, her recipes, and to watch the *Chef Baba Cooking Show*, please go to ChefBaba.com

Damir Perge

Born in Yugoslavia, Damir immigrated to the U.S. at the age of 11. He became a U.S. citizen at age 16 and represented the U.S. on the National Youth Soccer Team from 16 to 19. He was a McDonald's Soccer All-American and received a full soccer scholarship to play at Southern Methodist University, where he pursued studies in mechanical engineering.

Damir is an entrepreneur, former venture capitalist, author, screenplay writer, producer and complexity scientist. He ran a VC fund in Silicon Valley—focused on investing in the seed and early stages of the startup cycle.

As a venture capitalist, he raised more than $300 million for various companies and invested more than $50 million into 25 startups and early stage companies in the entertainment, publishing, media, sports, Internet, enterprise and consumer software, hardware, financial services, manufacturing, and transportation sectors.

He is co-founder of entrepreneurdex, a startup studio using complexity science to launch, accelerate and scale startups and growing businesses, and co-founder of Madman Pictures, a film and television production company. Damir is co-creator and producer of the *ChefBaba Cooking Show*.

Damir started as a cooking imbecile, but today he's proud to say he's Chef Baba's Sous Chef as he helps transfer Chef Baba's cooking and cultural knowledge from the old country.

Damir is an author of Entrepreneur Myths: The Startup Reality. His upcoming business books in 2018 include *Futbolpreneur: Football Thinking, Strategies and Methods Applied to Business and Life* (2018) and *The Art of War: Sun Tzu Applied to Business* (2018).

For more information about Damir, go to damirperge.com

Printed in the USA
CPSIA information can be obtained
at www.ICGtesting.com
LVHW062035270823
756437LV00010B/1351

9 780999 698419